Zest by Andy Davies

Published in the United Kingdom by Imje Tse Publishing

www.AndyDavies.online

Paperback ISBN: 978-1-7397291-0-3

Hardback ISBN: 978-1-7397291-1-0

Kindle ISBN: 978-1-7397291-2-7

First Edition

Zest

Leadership for a new generation of leaders

Andy Davies

Published by Imje Tse Publishing

For Cathy,
Shannon, Jessica, Harry, Josh,
George and Poppy. x

Contents

Foreword

For the first time in a long time, if not ever, Zest is a leadership book that opens with an invitation to explore, to actively practice and to continuously keep pushing the boundaries of one's own capacity, and not with a request to seek out or follow a prescribed solution or set of ideas. Andy brings a no-nonsense, caring and energetic desire to see the world of work shift gears and he offers a wonderful platform throughout Zest to help you, the next generation of leader, achieve that by learning from the present and the past, but also inviting the reader to imagine for themselves what good looks like in their context and bravely seeking to set themselves up for future success.

A refreshing, insightful and modern read, Zest is part strategy, part HR, part personal development, part organisational design but all with a very intentional focus on setting up the next generation of leaders for adaptable, holistic, commercially astute, human-centric and business success.

Andy does a wonderful job throughout Zest of modelling the future competencies that he signposts, such as empathy, adaptability and bravery, as he weaves powerful stories and data across a mix of practical case studies, personal interviews and 3rd party examples of less well known modern-day corporate heroes to bring his messaging to life for the next generation of leader.

Peppered with practical, real-life examples of leadership, what works well, what is too often missing and some blatantly poor and indeed shocking leadership examples of 'what to avoid', Andy offers a positively inviting, playful, to the point and exploratory approach to 21st century leadership and beyond in his new book Zest.

As an active corporate practitioner myself, I find Andy's 12 forward-looking competencies and his blueprint for future leaders not only compelling, but absolutely critical as we get used to navigating rapid change as business as usual. Andy does such a good job of weaving the critical hard competencies such as strategic thinking, networking and commercial awareness together with the necessary ascension and addition of critically important so-called soft skills (I prefer to call them humanistic skills or competencies) such as bravery, adaptability and empathy. To offer a framework by design that blends the whole human for personal, team, organisational and indeed societal gain, Andy is provocatively and bravely signposting a new, re-imagined way to review competency and one that is grounded in our whole humanity, not just in financial metrics that we all know are an outcome of getting the people stuff right.

Andy keeps the exploration throughout Zest super practical by offering a range of reflective and discovery questions as you make your way through the text. My invitation is to take the time to really digest, internalise and answer fully and honestly for yourself each question as I personally found real, practical value in doing so as a curious, seasoned leader.

Garry Turner
Curious explorer and founder of HEXO Change
Web - https://www.hexochangenow.com/
Linktree - https://linktr.ee/HexoChangeGarryTurner
Email - garry.turner@hexochangenow.com

Chapter 1

Introduction

When the boss confirms a line of action and immediately goes into the office of his or her own boss and delivers a contradictory message on behalf of the team, there is no love.
Yetunde Hofmann (Author)

The future of leadership is at a crossroads and you're stood right in the centre of it.

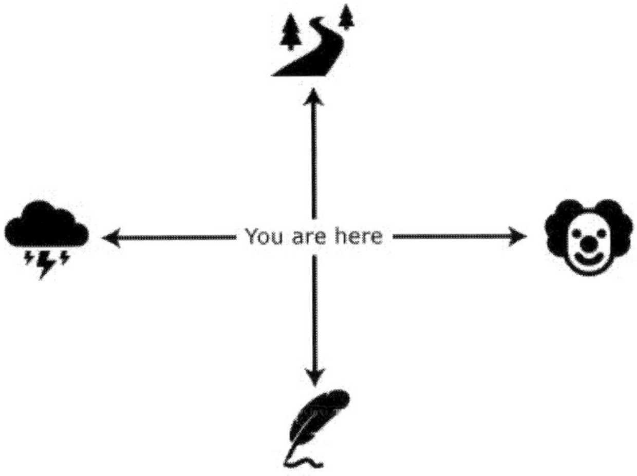

Behind you is leadership of the past – dictatorial, command-driven and centered on the few. You have three routes to choose from. To your left is a road which is like the past and many people have already progressed this way. You watch them move slowly with their shoulders hunched knowing they are just part of a machine. To the right is a road that is filled with fanciful leadership ideas that have been labelled as fads. There are many fads to choose from and change your mind on a regular basis so as not to let any one thing stick. This way you cannot be blamed if it does not work out. In front of you is a path where few people have ventured. The path is not well lit, it meanders like a river but there are voices calling you. They are telling you that it is ok to explore and to do something different to those around you. You have found the future of leadership and you just require the *zest* to go further.

Now is this time to focus on you – the future leaders who can lead businesses into the future of work. You can throw off the old beliefs and approaches and lead with charisma and vision supported by technology, increased mobility and a growing connectivity with people and markets around the world.

I want to help you find your *zest* for leading businesses of the future.

This book helps leaders and aspirant leaders to learn from real-world leadership examples and discussion, supported by research from leading institutions and practical advice from leaders and consultants. This gives the reader a basis to reflect on their current leadership approach and what is needed in the future. *Zest* refers to some theories for change management, leadership styles and culture. *Zest* bridges the gap between a deep theoretical textbook and the leader who is looking to learn from other leaders who have applied theoretical learning to different scenarios and, as a result, have a practical assessment of what worked and didn't work.

The case studies and examples are from global businesses including: Google, Amazon, CIA, Pay Group, Paravis Partners, Deloitte, Gravity Payments, Timpson's, Twitch, WeWork, Luckin, Nissan, Volkswagen, AOL, BP, Microsoft, McDonald's, Tumblr, Yahoo!, Thrive, Zappos, Netflix, Sony, Lenovo, Pixar, Adobe, Nike, Boeing, Facebook, Activision Blizzard, British Airways, British Olympic Association, Buurtzorg, Haier, Twitter.

The learning outcomes will be to help readers to:

- Understand what leadership competences are required for a leader in the current and future workplace.
- Appreciate how communication can affect the performance of a team.
- Consider how high performing teams are created and scaled.
- Appreciate how social media can be used by leaders to grow their personal brand.
- Develop their approach to change management.
- Consider how their leadership approach needs to change to keep pace with the changing environment.

Many books have been written on leadership; either from the theoretical perspective or from a biographical stance. *Zest* focuses on the everyday, practical side of leadership which is taken from experienced leaders and consultants who are supporting leaders to deliver change or business outcomes.

This book is for new and aspirant leaders looking to grow their leadership capabilities. If you have access to great mentors, then this should help you to have informed conversations about how to deal with different situations. If you're not in the fortunate position of having access to people who can help your grow as a leader then this book will help until you find someone.

As a new or aspiring leader, you can maximize the use of this book to help you become one of the leaders of your business, not by a title but by your actions. You should act as a leader with immediate effect. To help you develop your leadership ability, the chapters will help you to learn from current business leaders and reflect on the actions of failures in leadership so you can assess your leadership approach.

At its core, leadership is influencing others and great leaders are masters of social influence. They can administer power effectively by showing trust in their team that this power is seldom noticed. Effective leaders are good political actors who know the games to be played and how to manage political behaviour in a way that does not lead to group or organizational disruptions.

Leadership Tip

The impact of the global pandemic has shown that leadership matters more than ever, especially during unprecedented change. As a new leader you need to be able to lead people effectively through change by encouraging collaboration and commitment, providing a sense of purpose, sense building, and providing ongoing sponsorship. This will require energy, being present, but also being empathetic and compassionate which will help you to inspire and motivate individuals to trust and willingly engage with change in your organisation. Ultimately, leadership is about your approach and attitude and being able to motivate and engage people in change. If you are new to leading change then it is beneficial to find yourself a mentor to provide support and challenge.

Professor Julie Hodges, Durham University Business School

To start with, consider the leaders you work with and see in the media. Now think about an iceberg. What you see is their success and rewards. What you do not see is the hard work, failures, poor work-life balance, insomnia, disagreements, stress, missed opportunities and disappointment. Your job is to draw your own iceberg over the coming years and add the items above and below the waterline.

Before you read any further, I should let you in on three leadership secrets. Firstly, leadership is not just exhibited by the c-suite or directors. Leadership is an attitude that people display. The majority will walk past an opportunity but it is the minority who will see it, explore it and draw people together to exploit it. Leadership happens throughout the organization and any business that believes leadership is defined by grade or pay is a negative and stifling environment. Secondly, leaders aren't perfect. They are normal, fallible human beings who have feelings and get things wrong. Thirdly, you were not born a leader. None of us were. Instead, you must learn to be a leader and that takes hard work and time.

When you're reading this book, I want you to keep in mind the following questions:

- Why do you want to be a leader?
- How would you want people to describe your leadership?
- What would you want people to remember most about you as a leader?
- What do you fear about being a leader?
- Have you failed at being a leader and why?
- What would you describe as success for a leader?

These questions are designed to challenge you. I ask myself these questions on a regular basis. As time goes by, my answers change to some of them but some have remained the same for many years. I will not provide you with my answers as these will be deeply personal and you should explore your own thoughts on this!

Finally, congratulations on choosing a book that will give you the support and challenge you need as a new leader to develop your skills and lead your business into the future of work. Please complete the reflective activities at the end of each chapter and reflect on what you will take into your own leadership approach.

Andy

Part 1

The basis of great leadership

Chapter 2

Leadership competencies

"The irony of "soft skills" is that they're often the hardest to master. Leadership, communication, collaboration, creativity, and adaptability may not be technical, but they're increasingly vital. Behavioural, social, and emotional skills are what make humans indispensable."
Adam Grant (Organizational Psychologist & Author)

Introduction

If you have a Job Description, the chances are that it will contain a list of competencies you need to do your job. As leaders, these competencies will focus on communication, teamwork, delegation, customer service and achieving results. They are under-utilised, not measured, not reviewed for your job or for you and in short, a worthless collection of text.

Competencies should not be an afterthought or a box to fill on a job description template. When done correctly, they are an important part of selection, assessment and succession planning for some of the most important jobs in your business. They help to identify the behaviours you need from a person to be successful in a job and often have pen pictures to describe the scoring matrix that is attached to them. Measuring competencies requires time, effort and discussion. It is easier to identify what competencies are required for a job but you should not apply this same simplicity to a person. All businesses are different and there is no one size fits all. Leadership as a concept may carry similarities across sectors and industries, but it is vital to apply the unique finishing touches to each of the competencies on an individual basis. In this chapter, I will explore the key competencies required for our future leaders based on a changing world as what we expected before has now changed. (Hint: if your leadership competencies include 'time keeping' they are out of date!)

If you have not got as far as looking at a leadership framework then I will provide you with a foundation which can be applied and moulded to your own business. This framework is based on my own research, interviews with leaders and from articles which have also explored this subject. I have taken these resources and pinpointed which competencies future leaders require to be successful in a dynamic environment which demands more of leaders than ever before. Even after reading this chapter, if you decide that a leadership competence framework is not for your business, please take away some of the future leadership competencies and remember these when hiring your next leader. Understanding the benefits of these competencies will enable you to focus your questions and identify the right person.

Competencies in action

In 1944, the CIA[1] published the 'Simple Sabotage Field Manual' which provided local resistance fighters across Europe with guidance on how to weaken their countries by reducing production and efficiency at their plants and factories. They advised the managers should do the following:

- Insist on doing everything through "channels". Never permit short-cuts to be taken in order to expedite decisions.
- Make "speeches." Talk as frequently as possible and at great length. Illustrate your "points" by long anecdotes and accounts of personal experiences.
- When possible, refer all matters to committees, for "further study and consideration." Attempt to make the committee as large as possible — never less than five.
- Bring up irrelevant issues as frequently as possible.
- Haggle over precise wordings of communications, minutes, resolutions.
- Refer back to matters decided upon at the last meeting and attempt to re-open the question of the advisability of that decision.
- Advocate "caution". Be "reasonable" and urge your fellow-conferees to be "reasonable" and avoid haste which might result in embarrassments or difficulties later on.
- In making work assignments, always sign out the unimportant jobs first. See that important jobs are assigned to inefficient workers.
- Insist on perfect work in relatively unimportant products; send back for refinishing those which have the least flaw.
- To lower morale and with it, production, be pleasant to inefficient workers; give them undeserved promotions.
- Hold conferences when there is more critical work to be done.
- Multiply the procedures and clearances involved in issuing instructions, pay checks, and so on. See that three people have to approve everything where one would do.

This is the best incompetence framework I have seen - clearly setting out procrastination, deflection, inappropriate escalation and inappropriate delegation as key attributes towards helping to destabilise a business and ultimately, their country. What can be learned from this example is that without clearly setting out competencies that are regularly measured for leaders, incompetence's will grow and can be exploited by competitors. If you have read this guide on how to sabotage a business and recognise many of the behaviours from your own business, consider if your competence framework is working for you.

However, not everyone has a competence framework and those that do have one do not often have a separate framework for leadership roles. For many businesses, the cost of time, capacity, resources and knowledge are too great to justify the investment and they rumble along without a competence framework.

A further example of competencies in action is from a Public Sector client who wished to implement a new leadership competence framework. They had spent a small fortune on a big-name consultancy to help set their leadership framework and then set about measuring their senior leadership team against their new competencies. This investment in leadership heralded the new dawn of leadership in their organisation and they were keen to address the perceived gaps of the past. Like many Public Sector organisations, they were focussed on generating revenue and maximising income streams where previously they had not seized any initiative to do so. For these reasons, 'Commercial Awareness' had been identified as a leadership competence. I reviewed the scores from the assessments and discussed the outcomes with the Executive Director responsible for the transformation project. I explained that 'Commercial Awareness' had been the most poorly performing competence amongst the leaders and she should draw her attention to the Chief Financial Officer who had scored zero. They all knew he was against any form of change and wanted to bury his head in the sand until retirement, but this was a shock.

Despite the significance of this finding and the impact this could have upon the organisation, I was disappointed that they chose to sit on these results and did not take any form of action other than to send the individual on the same development programme as everyone else. This organisation knew about their competence weaknesses before an external assessor provided the evidence, but then they chose not to act. This decision slowed their rate of transformation and growth. The lesson I want to offer all leaders is that leadership competencies can be used to drive your business forward. This organisation failed to understand this and demonstrated that if you fail to use these insights to inform your strategic decision making, the competence frameworks themselves become redundant and should be cast aside immediately.

Bravery as a standout competence

My own survey of global leaders included whether bravery/courage is required by leaders. Bravery gained nearly a quarter of the votes which helps to reinforce that bravery is a part of being a leader.

One of the most under-rated competencies is bravery. As leaders, you are regularly called upon to make brave decisions, some of which with far reaching consequences. People often jump to military examples when they think of bravery in leadership, but this overlooks some of the closer examples of bravery in business which happen around us daily.

In his book 'Reboot', Jerry Colonna[2] discussed the decisions that were taken by a start-up business acquired by a venture capitalist. He explains that two months after completing the investment, the CEO called the investors to tell them that the business was failing. The CEO reviewed their position and pitched to the investors that dismissing everyone apart from himself and the CFO was the way to turn things around. They subsequently rebuilt the business themselves and two years later, went on to sell the business for five times the amount of investment. The bravery here was not only the CEO making the tough call to admit defeat and plan the re-emerging business strategy, but also by the investors to stand by two of the leaders who had got them to this position and believe in their solution.

Another fitting example is from Dani Polaner's[3] '7 Unicorn Drive' where he explains the story of Iza and Samo Login and their growth to a $1Bn business. From relocating to Cyprus to support their son, to engaging the KGB (now known as the Federal Security Service or FSB) to recruit a talented individual for their business, their story is full of bold, brave decisions. These decisions came with risk and uncertainty, but these brave decisions are fundamental to a leader when working to secure the future of their business.

On my podcast 'Leadership, the future and tea', the first podcast episode[4] was about bravery in leaders. Here is an extract of some of the discussion.

> *Deborah: Yes. You have to be super brave. And it's not the definition of brave that we've grown up with. It's not brave as in taking up a sword and running into battle. The bravery that we need is different. We need to be brave enough to be authentic, and to be human.*
>
> *Iain: But when you're in that ultimate leadership position, you're dealing with yourself. There's no way to hide. There's nobody to blame. It's the closest you ever get to truly understanding yourself and your individual weaknesses and your vulnerabilities and your frailties, and there is no shield left. I think that's why people talk about authenticity.*
>
> *Hiten: We always talk about the importance of being yourself, being real, being authentic, but as a leader, every single one of your thoughts, words and actions. have consequences. It's finding that balance. You can't just always do what you want,*

say what you want, say how you feel, you can't express that. You have a responsibility as a leader to do the right thing. And I think bravery is doing the right thing.

One of the first aspects to conquer in your quest to becoming a successful leader is understanding that you cannot do everything yourself. This demands bravery in trusting others and delegating, as it can feel vulnerable to expose yourself by delegating power and actions away from your control. There are two outcomes from this. Firstly, that it goes swimmingly, and you receive the plaudits for effective delegation. Secondly, if it goes badly, it can force you to reflect on questions such as 'Did I train this person properly?', 'Did I brief them properly and how was it received?' and 'What was the interpretation throughout the rest of the business?'. On a practical level, there is a degree of bravery required in delegating and this is often the first taste of bravery for a leader.

Now ask yourself, how do you test for bravery in a leader? What questions would you ask of a candidate to help understand if they could make brave decisions that could affect the future of your business? Or what scenario-based exercise would you give them to assess their bravery competence? Bravery is more difficult than many other competencies to assess and is best achieved by asking a candidate to provide examples of occasions when they have shown brave leadership which you can then explore through deeper questioning.

Resilience

In the same survey I conducted in 2021, resilience attracted the same number of votes as bravery/courage as another requirement for strong leaders. Psychology Today[5] defines resilience as '*the psychological quality that allows some people to be knocked down by the adversities of life and come back at least as strong as before. Rather than letting difficulties, traumatic events, or failure overcome them and drain their resolve, highly resilient people find a way to change course, emotionally heal, and continue moving toward their goals*.' For leaders, resilience is not about responding positively to one event but many events - probably in the same week!

For me, resilience is the competence that enables leaders to deal with setbacks, both minor and major, on a continual basis, and allows them to learn from these events and turn that learning into an energising force which enables them to achieve their goals.

When considering resilience in leaders, I am drawn to the example of Jeff Immelt, who took over from the legendary Jack Welch at General Electric (GE) in 2001 as the CEO. During his tenure, Jeff led GE through several global events including 9/11, the global financial crash of 2008 and the Fukushima nuclear disaster (GE built the reactors). During an interview, Jeff[6] talked about imposter syndrome and how leaders need self-reflection, self-confidence and self-renewal to overcome adversity when it feels most impossible. Jeff also identified that family, friends and coaches are also a key part in going home feeling like a failure but waking up with a renewed sense of belief in yourself. This demonstrates resilience in action from a former CEO of a global business with a workforce of around 300,000 people.

Adaptability

The competence of adaptability was another key result from my own research and attracted nearly half the votes in my survey. From personal experience, my continual postings in the military helped me to understand that adaptability was a key competence which would serve me well in the future, but this is something that is sadly lacking in many business people and professional organisations. To stand out from competition, businesses need to be able to pivot quickly to seize opportunities or to mitigate threats, and it is the adaptability of their people that make this possible. This requires a mindset of letting go of previous practices and processes. If you can also tailor your selection processes to ensure you are recruiting for adaptability, your business will benefit.

Leadership Tip

If you get chance to speak to people from your competitors, ask them if the competence of adaptability is widespread or even valued by the business. This will tell you a lot about their sense of readiness to react to the ever-changing environment.

What competencies are needed by our future leaders?

When I started to think about future leadership competencies, I look inwardly to determine the three words that I would use to describe myself. The first one I identified was 'connector'. What I mean by that is about relationship building between people and introducing people to others. Many leaders have failed in business by simply failing to connect with key people or influence changemakers, so if you are not already a connecter, today is the day to change your approach. Secondly, a 'futurist' is passionate about what the future holds; often seen as a positive person but it is a lot more than that. The excitement of it, the positivity, the opportunity, sitting down and thinking about the future and what we can do to influence it fuels this type of leader. The last one, and I have always believed in this from my first days in employment, is 'adaptability'. It brings me great joy personally to jump into different tasks daily and exercise this strength of versatility in leadership, whereas functioning in a repetitive way across decades is certainly not the mark of a future leader. Adaptability to move with the times is important for any leader and cannot be under-estimated.

During my many conversations with business leaders on my podcast, we discussed the competencies and traits required of our leaders. Here are their thoughts on what is required:

Mark Samlal, CEO and Founder, PayGroup Ltd

> *"So I would have to say without doubt, it really is for me and for mostly about passion. So if I can feel that passion, if I'm recruiting somebody, if I understand what they've achieved within the businesses that we know we have at Pay Group, then that's the first and foremost thing that even if it's unbridled passion, it's something that really resonates very well on myself. Because often in my early days as being a salesperson, I had my heart on my sleeve very often champion the cause. And that's something that makes me feel terrifically connected to somebody. Thereafter, it's really your ability to apply yourself to be able to complete and finish something. So you've got the passion piece, but you must have those skills to be able to complete and finish whatever it may be in life that you want to do. So the accountability attribute is very high. Passion, with the ability to complete and finish with a high level of accountability, self-accountability, are the really big things that I look forward to finding in my organisation with people or finding outside should they want to come to join us in Pay Group. It was something that I've always been coached upon. Definitely, by Phil and other leaders that if you've got the accountability matrix with inside of you, and if you've got the ability to complete and finish capabilities with yourself, and importantly, you've got the passion, then realistically, we can train anybody in whatever specific business requirements they may need to succeed. So we're not sending people to the moon at Pay Group. We don't need an aeronautical engineer to send people that distance. Through the passion every day and being able to communicate their passion effectively and concisely really helps with that. So I don't believe that it's changed over the years. It's been something I've always been strongly drawn to."*

Amy Jen Su, Managing Partner & Co-Founder, Paravis Partners LLC

> *"...their ability to think strategically and bring really good judgement. I think as you grow as a leader, as you take on more span of control, the decisions you have to make become incredibly nuanced and complex. So number one, a leader who brings judgement to say there's a grey zone here? And how do I think about the time horizon? How do I think about the impact on various stakeholder groups to get to the best decision or best*

answer is certainly not easy. So number one, would be that business judgement. Number two would be what we were just talking about the people leadership and the communication ability. As you grow in your career, there's a point where you realise even if you're the most phenomenal producer, you have to learn to work with others, or through others. And so that's a really key thing that you value others and getting worked on with others. And that you can communicate one to one, to Team one to many, as a leader. And then finally, the third trait that comes to mind, which I don't know, that we talk about often enough, is really leadership maturity, as we grow as we season, and I don't think this is chronological age, I think you can meet a 20 something year old earlier in their career and smell and sense that they have this but this is about self-awareness about self-regulation. And that even as you face challenge or tough decisions, you are not bringing your reactive self or what you think is in your own best interest or self-preservation. But again, you come back to those ethics and the integrity of trying to do what's right."

Yetunde Hofmann, Founder and Director, Solaris Executive Leadership Development

"Well, first of all, I believe that we all are leaders, I think whether you rule a nation, or you sweep the streets, or you sleep on the streets, we all are leaders, because we're making decisions. And leaders have a relational responsibility. It's all about relationships. So there are three key traits that I look for. The number one, the uber trait that I look for is the trait of love. And that love means that that acceptance of who I am, and acceptance of who you are, regardless of all your weaknesses. I may not agree with what you do, but I accept you as that human being that fundamental, unconditional acceptance of who you are. The second one is about contribution. Because I think that my job as a leader is to help another person's life be more successful. And your job as a leader is to do the same. And if we all asked 'How can I help you? What can I do to support you?' That's so key, how can I help you be the best you can be? So the attributes of contribution is key. That's the second one. And the third one, I think that which enables the other two, to flourish more is to have purpose driven leaders. When an individual has a purpose, and they understand who they are, why they're here, what they're here to do in business, what they had to do for their family, what they had to do for the community for society, then it allows them to think long term and think consequentially. Think 'How does how I behave impact the person beyond what I can see?' That's the third one."

Lori Niles-Hofmann, EdTech Transformation Strategist

> *"When it comes to leadership, and I even thought this before COVID, to me, a great leader has empathy. They're able to adapt or put themselves in the position of the people they lead. And I think any person cannot do that is doing a disservice because at that point, they're not leading, they're forcing. They need to have that ability to understand those feelings. I also really look to two aspects. I know a lot of people will say. You need to be underhanded to get to the top but I completely disagree. I have seen some people that I respect who made it to the top who made the tough decisions and done things because it was the right thing to do. And I have a huge amount of respect for them. And then the final one is actually malleability. And the reason I look to that is I really am impressed by leaders who have adopted and shifted their style and evolved. Maybe shifted but people, as circumstances have changed or as they've moved between organisations. They haven't just brought their standard leadership is this principle, but they're able to, again, have that sense of empathy and shape shift into being the leader that that team needs. They're not leading for the leader's sake, they're leading for the team."*

In 2015, Deloitte Poland[7] looked at the competencies leaders would require in the future in the context of a changing business need. Although focussed on the Polish market rather than a Europe-wide assessment, they identified a range of suggested competencies for future leaders. These included taking a broad perspective, a financial perspective, flexibility in action, leading change, building effective relationships, developing talent and exerting influence. These competencies align with many other studies and suggested frameworks, but it is their assessment of the top three competencies for board members that stands out. Deloitte identified that 'taking a broad perspective', 'leading change' and 'financial perspective' were the leadership competencies rated as most important for this level. This analysis should be of interest to any business who are seeking to review their competence framework. In my work I have referred to 'taking a broad perspective' as 'Strategic Thinking' and I have termed 'financial perspective' as 'Commercial Awareness'. These are often most lacking from senior teams yet are the competencies that are most likely to yield competitive advantage.

Further research from Deloitte[8], *Leadership for the 21st Century*, details leadership requirements based on their own survey of Global Human Capital Trends from 2019 and provides an in-depth analysis. The central point of the research is the need for future leaders to focus on technology and how they need to be 'tech-savvy'. However, the report showed that 81% of respondents identified the 'Ability to lead through more complexity and ambiguity' as a key requirement. I have always believed that the sign of a mature leader is their ability to deal with ambiguity. The ability to lead through ambiguity cuts across every sector and whenever I have worked, it is a simple test I have applied to the other leaders around me. With the level of change that is apparent in work and at home, it is important for leaders to be able to guide people through a turbulent environment. The success of their leadership through ambiguity can then be measured across the engagement levels of their teams, the turnover rates compared to similar teams in the same industry, their product/service output, the quality of their relationships with their customers and their willingness to perform a discretionary effort.

Leading through ambiguity can often be seen within the context of mergers and acquisitions, where CEOs are required to both manage this at a high level & ensure the overarching business message reassures employees around their stability once the change is complete. Both extremes of the business require leaders to step up and provide direction, and this all comes down to honesty and transparency. In these times, leaders also need to be confident in saying 'I don't know'. They also need to be proactive in finding out the answers and passing on as much information as possible to provide support and clarity on the future. It may be that the only clarity they have is a future date for a meeting or the public information that has already been distributed. Poor leaders will side with their people and refer to architects of the ambiguity as 'them'.

This will create an unnecessary distance from the issue and encourage people to spread misinformation. Poor leaders are easily spotted during times of uncertainty within a business. Indeed, they can often be people you least expect. Your role as a leader is not to be consumed by them and you should protect your own team from such poor leadership. Eventually, your business will need to deal with this poor leadership and if you have seen this within your own team, you must act to eradicate these leaders from your team. You should look to embrace those people who have shown the ability to lead through ambiguity and celebrate their capacity for future leadership as these are the people who need to be with you during the next period of ambiguity.

Future competence framework

In case you have missed what is happening around you, we live in a rapidly changing world which has tipped business on their heads in the last 10-20 years. This change has been caused by technological advances, increased mobility of people, emergence of global markets for previously local/national products and increasing automation which has shaken the traditional employment model. At the heart of these changes is technology. Moore's law[9] might have talked about the advancement of the speed of processing, but it is now the human and business outcomes of this prediction that we should concern ourselves with.

Leaders now work in an environment that is referred to as 'VUCA' (Volatile, Uncertain, Complex, Ambiguous). There is no respite from the constantly shifting economic environment and the people challenges faced 10 years ago are now overshadowed by completion from overseas businesses seeking to recruit remote workers. Where businesses were fixed in a host country with clarity on legislation, even small businesses now have operations in different regions with the need to an understand the laws of several countries.

CEOs now need to be experts in cultural awareness across the business but in previous years could remain isolated in their home country. Strategy needs to be tight enough to give direction to the business but loose enough to react quickly to unforeseen changes and opportunities. Marketing was talked about in terms of radio, tv and printed press coverage with the excitement of sponsoring a sports team. But now, digital marketing dominates the marketing approach and the rise of digital TV means that any business can now become an advertiser on a TV channel that serves their target audience.

All leaders are now accessible and contactable via social media platforms. Whether they are carefully groomed by PR staff or personally operated (Elon Musk), all leaders can now be contacted by their employees, shareholders, customers and partners.

Because of the VUCA environment we now work in, there must be a change to the leadership competencies that businesses have relied on thus far. What made our businesses successful in previous years will not stand-up to the future challenges we face and our leaders must change to cope with the new demands they face. If you have a competence framework, look at the competencies and the description of the competencies to understand if they are forward looking and sufficient for the business environment of today.

To provide a starting point for the future leader's competence framework, I have compiled all the leadership competencies gathered from my own research and interviews from over 480 responses, along with the leadership competencies that had been identified by other authors and researchers and created a word cloud to look at the consistently present competencies.

Figure 2.1 – Word cloud for leadership competencies

After I assembled the results and started to look more closely at the context and meaning that had been given to each of the responses, I landed on 12 leadership competencies that future leaders will need to be successful.

To help understand the value and context of these competencies I have organised them within the context of three clusters: leading the business, leading yourself and leading others.

I have built out a description for each competence along with a scoring matrix of 1-4 to show how these competencies could be measured by a business. The measurement should be graded against the job and the person, so the business can begin to understand how they measure up, identifying any gaps they may need to fill through personal development.

This clarity can also help recruitment, particularly for internal candidates, as they can measure themselves against the expected competence scores and identify a development path to secure their next job. It is important to remember than context is everything.

I have provided 12 competencies that are required by leaders of the future but if you wish to use this framework, you may determine that some jobs only need a selection of these competencies.

Figure 2.2 – The 3 clusters

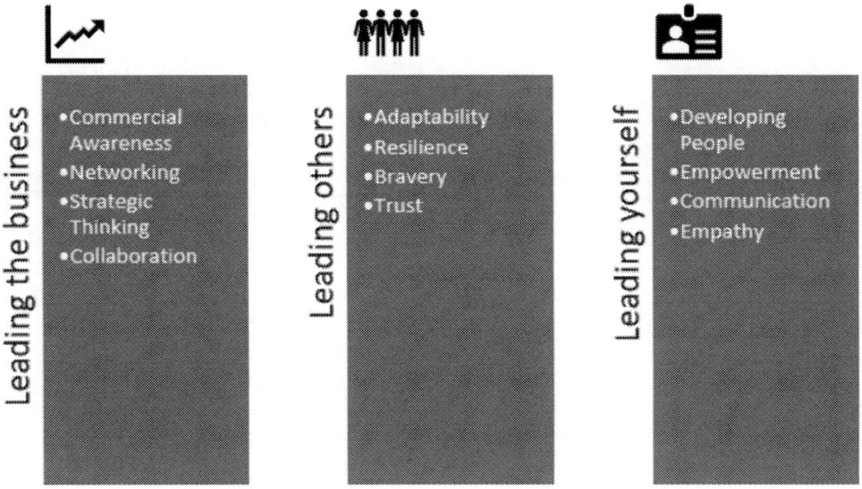

The following pages contain the description of the competence and a pen-picture of each level. I have identified 4 levels (1 is the highest, to 4 at the lowest) although you may wish to amend this further.

- **Leading the business**

Commercial Awareness	A leader must be able to understand the business impact of their plans and actions. This knowledge not simply about lowest cost options but extends further into the ability to assess partnerships for mutual value, seek opportunities to further the business outside of the normal routes and understand the time to cease effort on a project/partnership that is no longer adding value. This awareness spans countries and the ability to operate on an international stage in different currencies and with different legislation covering business operations.
Level 1	The leader is completely at ease leading complex commercial discussions to achieve the best outcome for the business. They are not fazed by the need to shift between the requirements of different countries and they are confident in dealing with suppliers, partners, customers and authorities. The leader actively seeks out opportunities to refine business processes and to improve the financial standing of the business. They consider all options open to them and they are acutely aware of the risks involved in any course of action they are taking and manage them accordingly.
Level 2	The leader has limited international experience but is seeking out opportunities to expand their commercial awareness through shadowing and mentoring. They have led smaller projects which have exposed them to some partnership work and given them the opportunity to review current processes to identify areas for improvement or areas to stop work. They are aware of their areas to improve and seek out new projects to expand their knowledge of different regions and how business is conducted in different countries.
Level 3	The leader has some commercial awareness but focuses too heavily on basic cost and value for money. Their thinking is limited to the traditional buyer/seller construct and they have little knowledge of partnership working. They show willingness to learn and understand more about different regions.
Level 4	The leader has limited commercial exposure and is either new to their role or lacks the confidence to take forward commercial activities for the business. They have some understanding of the business but little thought about challenging the current processes and are comfortable with others taking the lead.

Networking

A leader must be able to build networks before they are needed. This competence requires confidence and cannot be delegated to anyone else. They should actively identify the group of people they wish to meet before devising a sound strategy to achieve their global network. The ability to network is more than just exchanging business cards and relies on meaningful contacts through a variety of sources. A deep understanding of how to approach people and communicate in a way which initiates and encourages mutual contact is the hallmark of a good leader.

Level 1

The leader naturally engages with people from across sectors and national borders with ease. They are comfortable holding discussions with people they have just met to try and identify a common goal or shared contact. Not only do they network when there is a glaring opportunity to do so but they also create opportunities. They are experts at referring their own contacts within their network to help others benefit from the contacts they have made. They actively follow up with new contacts to reinforce their connection and ensure they grow through subsequent referrals by other connections.

Level 2

The leader has made great strides in growing their network and is starting to carve out opportunities to make contacts rather than relying on ready-made events. They have tried referring people within their network but have yet to master this approach for supporting people in their network. They have a basic strategy for who they wish to be in their network and they have made a start to achieve their aim. They have learnt from leaders who are experts at networking and they are keen to emulate their success.

Level 3

The leader tries to make new contacts within their network but is sometimes held back by their lack of confidence or their commitment to the need to network. They have seen other leaders expertly make contacts and build deep connections with people and aspire to achieve a higher level of competence. They have not yet explored all sources of networks and rely on just one or two sources to build their network.

Level 4

The leader is not confident about making new contacts and prefers to wait until people contact them. During a conference or business event, they make no effort to meet people from outside of their traditional network and if they do try, it is solely for their gain but not a mutual reason. When pushed to grow their network, their approaches to new contacts are ill thought out and without conviction.

Strategic Thinking	Leaders must be able to think beyond the confines of their business and look to the external environment to understand what is happening and how this could affect their business. They need to be able to assimilate complex information to formulate ideas, opportunities and identify threats to their business. This assessment needs to be a dynamic assessment that a leader can conduct rapidly while considering a range of actions. They should be adept at looking at a wide range of options and not be constrained by previous thinking. When they have assessed a situation and prepared their plans, they must then be able to present a complex issue in a simple way that ensures clarity amongst stakeholders. Their success will be their ability to make the VUCA world understandable and generate opportunities for their business.
Level 1	The leader is an expert in assessing the environment and quickly identifying both threats and opportunities for the business. They have honed their competence and are confident in their dynamic assessments and influence other business leaders in their planning. They present their thinking in a clear, logical manner with no room for misunderstanding and reduce complex issues to meaningful insights. The leader is focussed on delivering options to achieve success and takes a wide view to encompass possible actions by competitors. They are fearless in presenting their analysis.
Level 2	The leader possesses clear potential to deliver a coherent strategy to support the business outcomes but is aware they need more experience to meet the demands of the business. They may still be trying to conquer dynamic assessments but they show commitment to improvement and have a clear capability for strategic thinking. They can produce a range of options and provide good analysis of the situation.
Level 3	The leader attempts to look beyond the boundaries of their current work but they do not possess the ability to raise themselves from the operational workload to take a strategic perspective. They look to others for inspiration and will offer some basic level strategy, but this will be limited in analysis and impact. When they do present their insights, they are basic and not sufficiently clear for people to take immediate action.
Level 4	The leader's thinking is stuck in the past and they cannot move onto new ideas without substantial persuasion. They seldom seek out new opportunities and their lack of external awareness causes a sever risk of the business being left behind in the race for continual growth. The leader relies on others to provide the strategic thinking for them and is simply an implementer of strategy. Their lack of analysis is a risk to the business.

Collaboration	To be successful, leaders need to collaborate across their business. There is no room for self-isolation. Collaboration involves including people within projects to help share information, generate new ideas and provide a source of positive challenge to improve the overall outcome. Leaders should collaborate freely and without hesitation. This collaboration generates interest and support from around the business and helps build meaningful alliances with other departments. This can extend outside of the business to suppliers, customers, partners and other stakeholders who may be able to help deliver a project.
Level 1	The leader readily seeks collaboration across a wide group of stakeholders and includes external influencers who bring a different perspective. They listen carefully to their collaborators, seeking to understand their views and exploring how this could progress their initiative. Their active collaboration with other leaders builds strong alliances and delivers increasingly better outcomes for the business. They build a reputation as a trustworthy leader who can work across boundaries to deliver a positive outcome.
Level 2	The leader makes some attempts at collaboration but it does not come naturally to them. They have seen other leaders collaborate easily and they aspire to their level of confidence. When they do collaborate, they involve a variety of people and strive to build relationships with other leaders. They have had some experience of working across boundaries with the business and are looking for more opportunity to become fully proficient in this competence.
Level 3	The leader listens to the advice of others and seeks to collaborate in some projects. They are dismissive of the involvement of others but try to placate their stakeholders by showing some interest in the observations they bring. When they do collaborate with others, they limit their audience to people who will give an expected answer and will not seek to invite stakeholders who will provide positive challenge. They need to be pushed to collaborate although they know they need to improve their competence in this area.
Level 4	The leader prefers their own thoughts and does not wish to reach out to others for a fresh perspective. Their efforts to collaborate are contained within their team and are limited to one or two people. The leader does not actively seek collaboration with others and even when prompted will try to avoid the possibility of involving others. They are wary of outsiders and fear being embarrassed.

- **Leading yourself**

Adaptability	Adaptability supports many of the competencies in this framework as without it, all the work to scan the environment for threats and opportunities will be made worthless. This competence enables leaders to move easily between projects and switch focus. Adaptability not just about the leader making changes as an individual but about the need to understand that need for the business to adapt to survive and thrive. This may require some internal change but they recognise the value of not being stuck in one approach and readily move to capitalise on changes around them. Leaders are role models for adapting to the requirements of the business and the situation they are in. They act responsibly and lead their team by their actions. They exude confidence and set the vision for the need to adapt. Leaders challenge the norm and provide encouragement to adapt to colleagues in different departments.
Level 1	The leader easily adapts to the changing business environment and is an expert in bringing people along on the journey. They quickly assimilate a situation and understand how they need to adapt to address a threat or opportunity and set the vision for their employees. In doing this, they give confidence and reassurance to their team to adapt to new processes, people or places. They enjoy the challenge of adapting to an evolving environment and they continue to deliver business outcomes.
Level 2	The leader has shown the ability to adapt on many occasions but this is still an effort. They have led by example and their impact would be enhanced if their timing were better. They have identified other leaders who they wish to emulate and are working hard to understand how to turn insights into the need to adapt before it is too late.
Level 3	The leader is aware of the need to adapt but struggles to make this a reality for either themselves or their team. They often miss opportunities or are negatively affected by threats that could have been mitigated had they adapted earlier. Their employees may see some willingness to adapt but have been frustrated by their leaders' lack of speed to adapt. They are aware of their limitations but have yet to take direct action to develop their ability to adapt.
Level 4	The leader shows no will to adapt to a changing situation and continues to act in the normal way. They ignore the need to adapt and down-play the evolving situation that is driving the reason to adapt. They identify adaptability in other leaders and colleagues but struggle to incorporate their ways of working and behaviours into their own role.

Resilience	Resilience is a competence that is required in both the leaders and across the business to cope with the rapidly changing and uncertain environment. Resilience enables leaders to lead their teams positively during turbulent times and at the same time, protect their own wellbeing. Resilient leaders not only have a resilient mindset but also habits to help them build and mitigate difficult circumstances. Resilient leaders tackle adversity head-on and grow people around them to respond to issues they face. These leaders are easily identified as the 'go to' people in times of crisis as they have the presence of mind to look objectively at issues and provide the role model behaviours that others require to get through the situation.
Level 1	The leader is seen by others as a 'rock' during difficult times. They lead others effortlessly and display the behaviours expected of a leader during a crisis. They achieve this because they have developed a resilient mindset and the habits to support their personal resilience. Because of this, they are swift to see the need for change and act accordingly. They take charge of situations and turn threats into opportunities which they capitalise upon.
Level 2	The leader has made positive progress in their resilient mindset and the habits they have formed to cope with change and adversity. Their team has noticed a difference in their approach and they feel more confident about how their leader will get them through the next challenge they face. The leader has seen they can seize opportunities and deliver better business outcomes by being ready for uncertainty and volatility in their business.
Level 3	The leader has seen other leaders role modelling a resilient approach to change or adversity and recognises the need for this approach in their own leadership. They have started to explore a resilient mindset and how a leader can form unconscious and conscious resilient habits. They have tried to show greater preparedness and an ability to cope with a recent change or adverse situation and see some benefit from their previous coping mechanism.
Level 4	The leader has not adopted a resilient mindset and they do not possess any habits which enable them to cope with adversity or changing situation. Instead, they have unhealthy coping mechanisms which impact their team. Their resulting disappointment may lead to destructive behaviours for themselves, the team or the business.

Bravery

Bravery is required by leaders at all levels. Regardless of the size or importance of decision to be taken, leaders need to be brave and step out of the shadows to lead their team. Leading with bravery provides a role model to other employees and will inspire them to be brave in their work. Leaders will need to make changes and decisions on strategy, people or processes that shifts the business to a new focus. This could include severing ties with long-standing suppliers or entering a new market. Bravery does not come from poorly thought-out plans but from carefully considered options which mitigate risk. Once the options are clear, a brave leader can be clear on their way forward.

Level 1

The leader constantly acts bravely to act which enables the business to grow and seize opportunities they have identified. They are the role model for other leaders to follow and their employees see a high-performing leader. The leader is the centre-point for business strategy and they are consulted by other leaders who are seeking endorsement of their decisions.

Level 2

The leader has gained confidence and strives to act bravely when looking at opportunities and threats to the business. They are seen as a growing leader who understand the need for bravery in their decisions. The leader is supported by a mentor to grow their ability and confidence.

Level 3

The leader occasionally shows some bravery but this is only with the support of other leaders. They have yet to find their own way to act bravely and miss opportunities as they take too long to act.

Level 4

The leader does not see they need to be brave and instead seeks to follow in the footsteps of others so they can detach themselves from decisions. When asked to make decisions or changes, they pass the responsibility to another leader.

Trust	Leaders generate trust within the business through their actions. This competence is about being trusted and trusting others to do their job. It is a component of a good culture and must exist for a business to flourish. Leaders can establish trust by small actions and then build on this. This competence is closely aligned to empowerment and will be relied upon to achieve many outcomes for the business.
Level 1	The leaders seek to build trust and be trusted at every opportunity. They reassure people that they are confident in their abilities and support employees who are not experienced at working in a high-trust environment. The leader is often sought by the business to lead great projects as trust is a bedrock of their leadership toolkit.
Level 2	The leader has grown their confidence and has started to role model trust within their team. They are noticed within the business and are starting to be involved in projects that were reserved for other leaders who were trusted. They have sought mentoring and support to grow more quickly as a leader and recognise this is a key competence for them to develop.
Level 3	The leader has attempted to grow trust within their team and has made some efforts to support employees to grow. They are not yet comfortable with widening the trust they have given to people and still try to deal with fine details rather than trust people to execute an agreed plan.
Level 4	The leader shows little trust in their team and does not seek to grow trust. They prefer to undertake all actions themselves and are often referred to as a micro-manager. This lack of trust affects their overall ability to lead and they are paralysed when the leader is not present.

- **Leading others**

Developing People

Leaders should seek to develop others and in turn, create new leaders. This interest in development should be key for the leader and they should help people understand that they are responsible for their own development. A leader's role in this is to help people identify their own development needs and then support them in securing the resources to achieve this development. Successful leaders will help their people develop by acting as a role model for development and constantly seeking to learn. Great leaders are comfortable not knowing all the answers but own the responsibility to develop into better professionals.

Level 1

The leader places development of their people at the heart of their people strategy. They believe in the need for continual development for both personal growth and as a route to competitive advantage. They help people understand the future direction of the business and the implications for personal development. The leader is a great role model of personal development.

Level 2

The leader has a growing understanding of the need to develop their people and has made some steps to support their team. They would like to support more development within their team but have not yet managed to connect the outcomes of development with the business strategy. They have completed some personal development and recognise some of their team would benefit.

Level 3

The leader has shown some awareness of the need for personal development but this has been driven by other leaders imposing the need for development. They are not self-starters and when pushed, will support people on their team. They have conducted some personal development but only when they are pushed to attend.

Level 4

The leader does not provide support to develop their people and views the development of their team as a threat to their position. They believe they do not need any further development themselves and show no commitment to grow their own knowledge or act as a role model.

Empowerment

Leaders should seek to empower their team to deliver results as this fosters confidence within other leaders. Empowerment is a sign of trust and moves a leader to a more strategic position. Empowerment is also a sign of maturity of a business which enables a business to move quickly as decision making is accelerated. Leaders who have successfully achieved a fully empowered team are free to explore new strategic initiatives which makes them stand-out from their peers. Other leaders will look to empowering leaders as a source of inspiration.

Level 1

The leader has full confidence in their team and has built clear boundaries for action. The team understands they are empowered to act within the boundaries and they have the full support of their leader. The leader enjoys the speed the team can act, the ability to explore strategic issues and can evidence business outcomes which have been achieved because of their empowered team.

Level 2

The leader has built a solid team and foundations on which they can empower their team. They have seen success and gained confidence from their initial efforts to step back and trust their team. They need to focus on even greater empowerment to achieve the increase in speed of decision making which will lead to better business outcomes. Their team can see a real difference and enjoy the trust placed in them.

Level 3

The leader has tried to empower their team but lacks the confidence that this will work. They easily fall back to micro-managing each project and quickly undermine any confidence the team may have built. They see some team members as a threat to their position if they empower them to act.

Level 4

The leader likes to manage everything within the team and wants to be the focal point for everyone. They feel they are unable to take holidays as the business will fail without them. They have little confidence in their team to complete the processes they have created and the team feel unable to act without expressly being told to do so.

Communication	Leaders should communicate freely with the team and seek to instil a transparent attitude within the business. Withholding information is the exception reserved only for highly sensitive matters. Leaders are available to discuss topics with all employees and create a sense of approachability. When asked questions, they are comfortable with difficult messages and seek to reassure people where necessary. Leaders will employ many tactics of communication and not rely on one channel. Not only will they communicate widely but they will also seek to ensure their message has been received and interpreted properly. They are comfortable communicating to all audiences - internal and external.
Level 1	The leader is recognised by their team and the business for the environment they have created where everyone has a voice. They share information freely amongst the team and grow trust based on the information they have shared. They are adept at shaping their message and channel based on the communication they wish to achieve. The leader is a role model throughout the business and can be relied upon to be an ambassador for the business both internally and externally.
Level 2	The leader employs a range of methods to communicate and has gained confidence in their competence after several good results from open communication. They have yet to master the art of selecting the right channel for the message they wish to communicate but they are keen to develop. They seek out opportunities to represent the business internally and externally to build the reputation and communication competence.
Level 3	The leader attempts to communicate with their team but is unsure of the level of information they can share within their team. When they do communicate, it is by one favoured channel and they do not to seek to understand if the information has been correctly received. They see the efforts of other leaders and wish to communicate better throughout the business.
Level 4	The leader is isolated from their team and avoids communicating with them. If asked a question, they tend to deflect or avoid providing an answer. They are regarded as introverted and can often be seen as under-confident within the business. The leader fails to inspire the team through their lack of communication.

Empathy	Leaders show empathy when they genuinely try to understand what others are experiencing and feeling. Leaders who show true empathy listen intently and notice non-verbal cues. Empathetic leaders easily build relationships with other people around the business and in the customer base. These leaders are also better at keeping employees engaged and delivering excellent customer experience. Empathetic leaders move easily between different situations (including cultures and countries) and with a diversity of people. They are successful in any of these situations as they listen, build relationships and understand the situation of other people.
Level 1	The leader is exceptional at listening to people and understanding a variety of situations. They do not seek to judge or provided unwanted solutions. They build engagement with a wide audience and gain the trust of many people. They are not self-serving and instead seek to provide support and guidance based on the discussions they have held.
Level 2	The leader has successfully built an engaged team through their empathetic approach but still lacks the confidence of an experienced leader to be empathetic without clearly showing they are trying. They have had some experience in adopting their approach to either cultures or countries and understand the benefits that can be gained.
Level 3	The leader has made some attempts to listen to their team members but steps in too early with proposed solutions to their perception of a problem. They have not successfully built engagement but their team see they are trying to understand the situation.
Level 4	The leader shows no concern for other people and cannot understand what others are experiencing. They do not attempt to understand others or that different situations may require a different approach. They show no energy to work with a diverse range of people.

Using the framework

To make more use of the framework, you should assess the job and score each competence and then score the individual within the job against each competence. This gap analysis will provide a clear indication of developmental areas.

Figure 2.3 – Competence gaps

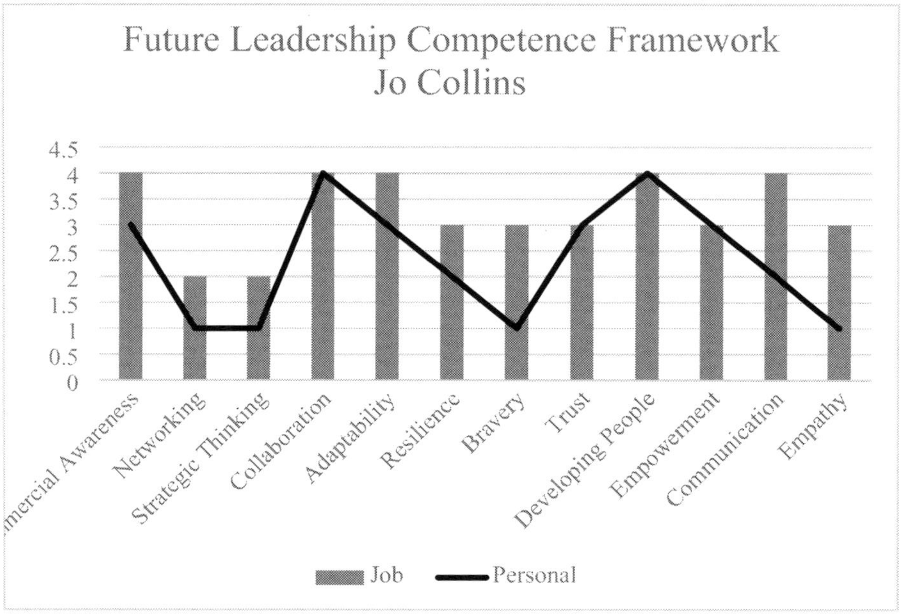

In the above example for Jo Collins they have several competencies where the job requirements exceed their personal scoring (Commercial Awareness, Networking, Strategic Thinking, Adaptability, Resilience, Bravery, Communication and Empathy). If this information is not acted upon, the future leadership competence framework is merely an expenditure of time that delivers no benefit. Businesses need to be able to support people to grow their competence in these areas to attain the level of ability the business has deemed necessary for the operation of the job.

Now you have seen the future leadership competence framework, it is time to review what you ask of your leaders. If you already have a leadership competence framework then take the opportunity to review it considering the competencies I have highlighted in this chapter. Some of your competencies may be the same but are they focused on the need for the future of work and what we need from our leaders? Part of your research may be to look around your industry to seek help from other businesses about what leadership competence framework they have in place. There are many examples of frameworks available online which may help your assessment of your own framework but the future leadership competence framework is already based on research of the requirements of future leaders.

You now have the information to review your existing leadership competence framework or to implement the one I have described.

Before doing this consider what you are trying to achieve, what senior buy-in exists for this to happen and if you have the in-house expertise to support the implementation.

Summary

A business can create a competitive advantage by setting standards for leadership competencies and making a commitment to developing people who will become future leaders for the company. Mentorship, guidance and shadow opportunities support the role of the leader, a role in which individuals build on experience and shape their own best practices for leadership tasks. By focusing on developing these competencies, the business will be able to foster better leadership among its employees and build future leaders, both for the future and for the current workforce.

Reflective activities

- Understand if your business has thought about the competencies your leaders need to support the future of the business.
- Review your recruitment and selection activities to ensure they actively look for the competencies you require.
- Explore how you identify gaps between the required competence and the person's level of competence. Is this robust or is it based on chance?

Suggested reading

- Colonna J. (2019). *Reboot: Leadership and the Art of Growing Up*. Harper Collins. New York.
- Polajnar D. (2021). *7 Unicorn Drive*. Login5 Aphrodite Ltd. Cyprus.

Chapter 3

Leadership approach

"There are only two ways to influence human behavior: you can manipulate it, or you can inspire it."
Simon Sinek (Author)

Introduction

Today is a new age for leaders. What we did five or ten years ago, and thought was appropriate leadership, is now old. We now have a workforce with five generations of people, where retirement is an event that happened to previous generations and where the newer generations expect different opportunities throughout their career which does not have a prescribed end date. What an incredible time to lead.

There are two major factors that have affected the approach we need to lead with. These are the internet and increased global mobility. Twenty years ago, when I bought my first book from Amazon, I had no idea what a behemoth it would become and I didn't really consider the impact the internet would have on my leadership approach. The speed and ubiquity of the internet has freed people to learn new skills, take more control of their lives and seek out new opportunities. It has given people the ability to look for roles they never knew would exist and then supports them in discovering more about companies than they ever thought about. At the same time, fuelled by the availability of travel through the internet, global mobility for people has become easier than ever before. The jet-age of the 1950s & 60s may have opened more destinations, but the internet has opened opportunities.

This now means that even the smallest company operates in an international market for both goods and people. If one of my team is unsettled at work, they have a clear opportunity to apply for a job anywhere in the world whilst not leaving their chair. The package I now offer people is in competition from global competitors and not just the local rivals. My leadership performance is assessed and critiqued through online platforms such as Glassdoor and I am judged by prospective candidates against this.

Now is the time to consider your leadership approach and learn from others around you. In this chapter we will examine the leadership of others through case studies, an assessment of the mini-series Chernobyl and other recollections of leadership success and failure.

Who are the real leaders?

Have you ever stopped to look around your business and consider who are the real leaders? Leaders do not need fancy titles and big offices. They are leaders because of their attitude. These people exist at all levels of a business and as a leader yourself, you should make it your task to find out who these people are. Here are a few pointers to help you spot them:

- They are often the quieter people who seldom seek the limelight.
- They are the people approached by others as a source of guidance.
- They endorse change and others quickly adopt change.
- They ask questions.
- They seek to improve.
- They build networks.
- They connect people.
- They continually learn.
- They see feedback.
- They show integrity.

Now consider how you are a leader. Each business has a different approach to assessing their employees and leaders. Often these are rooted in 'employee satisfaction' surveys, 360 assessments, Gallup polls or whatever the new fad is that results in a colour being assigned to a person (Hint: it is the same thing but just repackaged). The most important part of these assessments, including online reviews, is where it speaks about the leader. As a leader, I want to get the feedback so I can improve, and never let anyone tell you there is no room for improvement.

Leadership in action

Can you remember what you were doing on 26 April 1986? I doubt many of us can remember with absolute certainty, but this was a key date in the history of humanity, the date of the Chernobyl disaster. For many of the people involved in this crisis, they have been forced to recount their experiences many times over so we can learn what happened and how to prevent such a disaster from happening again. The 2019 HBO mini-series of the disaster, 'Chernobyl'[10], and its aftermath, provides a great opportunity to assess the leadership of the key characters. (I accept this is a television programme and that some parts of it were enhanced for the screen, however, the actions of the characters are what is assessed and not the historical accuracy.) The following five examples of leadership failings reveal the true approach of leadership from the two most senior leaders at the plant. Consider if you recognise any of these traits from your experience:

- Anatoly Dyatlov (Deputy Chief Engineer) is pictured trying to understand what just happened within the reactor building. After some pointed questions to his team, he turns to the senior operator and states "I am going to the Administration building to call Fomin and Bryukhanov. I do not know if I can make this better for you, but I can make it worse." At this point, Dyatlov does not know the cause or the extent of the issue but he has started to attribute blame, undermine the expertise of his team and make threats. This leadership approach has nothing to do with the severity of the situation and already points to a climate of fear in the control room. This introduction to the leadership approach at the plant is reinforced when Viktor Bryukhanov (Plant Director) arrives at the Administration building where Nikolai Fomin (Chief Engineer) is waiting for him outside. Upon Bryukhanov's arrival, Fomin greets him with "Whatever the cause, you nor I can be to blame." At this point, the executive team at the site are manoeuvring themselves away from any accountability for the issue that has occurred.

- The conversation continues inside the Administration building as Fomin assures Bryukhanov that no-one can blame him for the accident. Bryukhanov snaps back "Of course no-one can blame me for this, I was sleeping." The pushing of blame continues between Fomin and Dyatlov as they both established that they were running the tests that had been approved and supervised by each other.

- When presented with the evidence of a high meter reading by one of the plant operators, the trio of Dyatlov, Fomin and Bryukhanov all immediately moved to belittle his expertise and dismiss the evidence he presented. Instead, they continued to discuss Dyatlov's incorrect theory for the accident as if this was fact. This cumulated in the trio getting angry with the plant operator when he advised there was graphite on the ground as they advised him that "You didn't see graphite on the ground because it's not there." They are now clearly bullying the operator and using their positions as forcibly as possible whilst unwilling to hear the truth. These actions are not leadership. This is face-saving panic by executives who need to lead now more than ever before.

- In contrast, Valery Legasov (First Deputy of the Kurchatov Institute for Atomic Engineering) is seen in a meeting with President Gorbachev challenging the interim report that has just been presented to the meeting. Legasov refuses for the meeting to be adjourned and ignores the request from Boris Shcherbina (Deputy Chairman to the Council of Ministers, USSR) to take the discussion away from the committee. Instead, Legasov is brave, honest and gives a clear assessment of the level of radiation at Chernobyl. He uses his expertise to dismiss the untruths that are being exchanged about the level of radiation and that the impact will be greater than has been presented in the report. Legasov continues to exhibit sound leadership as he once again challenges the authority of Shcherbina in a helicopter. As they approach Chernobyl, Shcherbina orders the pilot to fly over the reactor core so he can see inside. Legasov steps in immediately to tell the pilot to ignore the order or they will all die. Legasov knows that by countermanding this order he is placing himself in immediate risk of sanction by Shcherbina, but he knows the impact of the order on all the crew and passengers. His intervention is successful, and they avoid flying over the reactor.

- Fomin and Bryukhanov meet Shcherbina at the helipad where he has just landed with Legasov. Upon meeting Shcherbina, Bryukhanov hands him a list of the people that he thinks are accountable for the incident. This action is the continued apportionment of blame that has been a theme for Fomin and Bryukhanov since their arrival in the story. Even after Fomin has been dismissed by Shcherbina, he is led away by the guards but still announces that "Dyatlov was in charge".

Both Legasov and Shcherbina then continue to lead the disaster recovery efforts and to avoid further explosions, they identify a need for three divers to enter the plant room under the reactor to open a sluice valve. The meeting with the divers is tense as Legasov and Shcherbina explain the task. Legasov is open and honest with the divers explaining the risks involved and the outcomes of not conducting the work. They discuss the monetary reward and promotion that is available, but Shcherbina is clear that this carries significant risk, and they cannot be certain of the outcome for the divers.

Nothing is held back and both Legasov and Shcherbina are holding a fully transparent discussion with the workers. They answered the questions posed to them as openly as possible. How different would the outcome of this meeting had Fomin and Bryukhanov led the meeting? Three divers stepped forward and successfully opened the sluice valve saving a much wider catastrophic explosion which would have affected much of Eastern Europe.

During times of pressure, people act differently. There is no surprise here. What we saw in 'Chernobyl' were leadership failings where the people who had led the engineers to a disaster were then leading through a blame culture. When the scrutiny arrived in the form of Shcherbina and Legasov, two of the major contributors to the explosion (Bryukhanov and Fomin) exposed themselves as failed leaders who had identified the people who were accountable.

When Shcherbina started to question the assertions made by Bryukhanov and Fomin, the final failure leadership occurred as Bryukhanov listened to a question and then turned to Legasov and asked, 'Why can the Minister see graphite on the roof?'. This final act of abdication also signalled the end for Bryukhanov and Fomin as they are dismissed by Shcherbina. In these few words, Bryukhanov had distanced himself from Fomin and had thrown him under the bus.

Strong leaders do not act this way. They accept failings and look to improve whilst supporting those around them. Even during times of pressure or ambiguity, real leaders step up to absorb the distractions and difficult moments so people around them can deliver the outcomes that are required. As a leader, this is my responsibility to my team. What role do you play in your business? Are you Bryukhanov or are you Legasov?

Servant Leadership

Is there a leadership school of thought that you have bought into? I have never really been a subscriber to one approach, instead considering elements of different leadership approaches and theories to forge my own path. In the last three years, I have been following and reading more about servant leadership, which as a concept has some great connections with the actions and behaviours of many successful leaders.

Servant Leadership was developed by Robert Greanleaf[11] in the 1970's. He developed this idea after reading Hermann Hess' 'Journey to the East'[12]. In this story, a secret order, the League, has sponsored an expedition to the East containing a storyteller referred to as H.H. and another member of the League. Included in the group of travellers was Leo, the servant for the group. Throughout the trip, he kept people supported, motivated and has an extraordinary presence. Eventually, Leo left the group and the journey is abandoned.

Years later at the secret order, H.H. realised that Leo was the leader of the order that Leo was leading the expedition whilst acting as the servant. H.H. noted that as a leader, Leo was never seen except when needed and was unassumingly friendly. In 'Journey to the East', Leo explained to H.H. the law of services which he summarized as "He who wishes to live long must serve, but he who wishes to rule does not live long."

The servant leadership approach is not just confined to a book and has real relevance in modern business. When asked what advice he would give to people who are new to leadership, Skip Marshall, CEO at InTech Ideas, said:

> *"Be a #servantleader. Servant Leaders put their #peoplefirst.*

Focus on building trust with your team and empowering them to be successful. Although a bit oversimplified...managers tell people what to do...servant leaders clear obstacles for their team."

This is an example of some great advice from an experienced CEO.

Servant Leadership is talked about more now than ever before and I attribute this to the fact that it is rooted in the people aspect of leadership. In a Harvard Business Review article, Dan Cable[13] described that 'servant-leaders have the humility, courage, and insight to admit that they can benefit from the expertise of others who have less power than them.' The rise of servant leadership has increased at the same time as many influencers, such as Garry Turner[14], host of the podcast 'Value through Vulnerability', have increasingly discussed about the vulnerability of leaders. (More recently Garry has started HEXO Change which you may wish to explore on YouTube[15].) Accepting that you do not know or that you are wrong as a leader is not something that is taught. Showing this vulnerability and having less power than people around you moves straight towards Servant Leadership and the benefits it can bring.

Cable offers three pieces of advice for people to get started on the Servant Leadership journey. Firstly, he advises people to ask how you can help employees do their own jobs better. Secondly, listen to your people which will help to create low-risk spaces for employees to think of innovative ideas. Thirdly, be humble. My additions to this advice are to ask people what can I do help them and what do they need to be successful in their job? By now, you should be connecting this approach with some of the competencies mentioned in Chapter 2, such as trust and empowerment. You will also see other traits of servant leaders within the following chapter which include leading by example, developing others and openness to new ideas.

Examples of servant leaders include Mother Theresa, Martin Luther King, and George Cadbury. More recent examples include Fed-Ex[16] and their belief in 'People-Service-Profit'. The outgoing CEO of Starbucks, Howard Schultz[17], described his successor Kevin Johnson as a true servant leader, whilst Marriot International have a 'people first' mantra.

They state in their Core Values & Heritage website that they will 'take care of associates and they will take care of the customers.' Servant leadership is not a small idea for small businesses or niche leaders. It has reached into large multi-national corporations and the thinking of high-profile leaders. If you have not heard of this approach before, you now have the background and opportunity to learn more about a basis of leadership that could underpin your future leadership style.

Case Study – Servant Leadership in action – Mr Umesh Raja

Hiten Bhatt, Leadership Coach and author of 'The leadership adventure'

https://www.linkedin.com/in/hiten-bhatt/
https://leadershipadventurebook.com/

The great Greek philosopher Aristotle once said, "educating the mind, without educating the heart is no education at all" Aristotle was pointing out that education has a role much bigger and much more important in society than developing intellectual people, it must also develop worthy people. When I was asked to think of a leader who exemplifies servant leadership in action, the humble and considerate, Mr Umeshchandra Raja came to mind.

Mr Raja was a headteacher of The Swaminarayan Independent School in London. During his 19 year tenure, the school was recognised for its numerous achievements. In 2010, the BBC ranked the school 23rd in the United Kingdom for best GCSE-level results in the school league tables. The average GCSE points per student at the school was a 609. In the same year, the Daily Telegraph ranked the Swaminarayan School second in the country based on the league of tables of independent schools.

During the course of his great career, Mr Raja has achieved many accolades, having completed his national professional qualification of headship (NPQH) in 2003, he has gone on to become an inspector for the ISI (The Independent Schools Inspectorate). ISI is appointed by the Secretary of State for Education to inspect association independent schools. It is a leading UK and overseas independent school inspectorate.

Mr Raja was one of the first Indian inspectors to have achieved the accolade and he regularly travels to inspect British International Schools all around the world. He has travelled to inspect schools in Panama, Hong Kong, Egypt, Spain, Nigeria and Kenya to name just a few. As a leader, with a vast array of experience in managing, leading and supporting people and the challenge of running a highly successful independent school, his thoughts on leadership are thought provoking and useful to businesses and anyone looking to develop a more people centred approach to leadership.

Nearly all schools are run on a not for profit basis and great educators take pride in working on behalf of the public good but schools are in fact still businesses. Businesses operate by providing a product or service to their customers. Schools operate to provide an education (a service) to students (customers). It is this very interesting juxtaposition between the valuable contribution educators make to society and the fact that schools are still run as businesses that call for a different type of leadership, a servant leader. Below are some of the questions I asked Mr Raja about his career and leadership lesson's he has learnt along the way.

Bhatt: What motivated you to become a teacher?

Raja: When I was studying in a Primary school in Mombasa , Kenya , I always found history and maths quite challenging. When I was 9 years old, we had this amazing history teacher who joined our School. She brought history alive. Being creative and always bringing a story element into her teaching meant there was never a dull moment. It was also her passion and enthusiasm that shone. She made sure that not only every child passed the history exam but also ensured that they excelled in the knowledge of the subject by developing a love for history.

School was from Monday to Friday. Every other Saturday, she would volunteer her services and invite a group of students at her own home for extra sessions to those students who needed them and to any other students that were interested.

These sessions were highly engaging and she never put any students down or use any discouraging language for their lack of knowledge and skills. In fact, she was always motivating and encouraging. I was astonished at her proficiency in delivering lessons to a very high standard. What stood out for me, first and foremost about this teacher was that she absolutely genuinely cared about her student's progress. She would sacrifice her own time at the weekend and ensure that any additional support anyone required was provided. This teacher went the extra mile for me and other students. She impacted not only our results but also raised our self-esteem.

Looking back on this now, I realise that this was for me a significant moment in my life. I felt inspired to one day become a teacher and also enthuse children to reach their full potential but more so provide care and empathy. Similarly, it was not until my secondary school in Mombasa, when I really grasped the basics of the mathematics. I actually enjoyed the subject as we had an exceptional maths teacher who too gave up his own time and effort during lunchtimes or after school in ensuring that not only did we understand the concepts but also used the subject in a practical real life context. Above all, he cared. That was highly significant for me. I felt both of these teachers were not required to spend the extra time and energy supporting students, however, they went above and beyond the call of duty of what one would typically expect from a teacher. These two highly dedicated teachers inspired my decision to take up a career in teaching. Later on in my education, I was accorded with a degree in maths and was also awarded a teaching qualification PGCE to teach Secondary maths.

Bhatt: What has been your approach to leadership?

Raja: Lead from the front.

Sir John Dunford, said that successful leaders at all levels need four H's: Hope, Humanity, Humility and Humour and someone that knows how to "water the plants."

Wherever I have worked I have always been child centred. My beliefs are that leaders should absolutely lead from the front and get involved at every level whenever required. In one of my first jobs as Headteacher at Abbey Primary School in Leicester, there were times where I felt that the tasks I wanted to have happen were not happening fast enough. I remember staying back at the end of the school day ensuring children's work was prominently displayed and changed at regular intervals. New work was put on the display board every half term. Once, I remember that the school contractors had not painted my classroom door and some walls. With the help of a few of my friends, we painted the walls and the door. I was told by other teachers that it was not in my job description but how long could the children wait to see the wonderful environment within the classroom and their work being acknowledged and the feeling of self-worth so as to feel energised. It was no ordinary classroom. It was a place for solace for them this is where I think leaders come into their own. When you care about something as a leader the responsibility for making that change begins and ends with you.

As a leader, I think it is important to be a role model and be willing to take on any tasks, menial or not that need to be done. If a table, bench or chair needed moving, I didn't ask anyone to move it, I just got up and sorted it out myself. Rolling up the carpet, clearing the stage or stacking up the chairs were things that I was never hesitant of doing despite being the leader. The mindset is that your role or position should not stop you from doing any task just because you are the boss. You have to put your ego to the side as a leader and be willing to muck in and this sends a positive message to the team and challenges the "it's not my job' mentality that holds back so many teams from being more productive. When people see the leader getting involved and on the ground they are also more willing to put in the extra effort. True leadership is the ability to influence, inspire and help others become their best selves, building their skills and achieving goals along the way.

Invest in your team.

Leaders are nothing without their team and very early on in my career, I realised the importance of investing in my team and appreciating everyone within the school community. I always put an emphasis on team building activities, socials as well as formal training opportunities to develop leaders. I think it is really important for members of a team to bond well and so for my staff, I always took time out to organise things like, go kart racing, bowling, meals not just at Christmas but regularly throughout the year. My beliefs are that through team building, one connects the members of a team and strengthens the relationship between them and this should be ongoing process that helps increase loyalty amongst each other.

The Swaminarayan School's motto was "in the joy of others lies our own" it was the life message of my Guru his Holiness Param Pujya Pramukh Swami Maharaj and was woven into the DNA of our school in everything we did, and one of our most important values was service. Teachers and students alike were given regular opportunities to serve the community in many ways, whether that was serving the elderly, cleaning the local park and surrounding environment or our regular fundraising activities. I passionately believe that serving the community and especially those less fortunate than ourselves is something that every student should take away from their education not just the academic skills of maths or English but values that make one a better citizen in a society that seems at times to be growing more and more self-centred by the day.

Leaders should get to know their people.

I believe that leadership is about being connected with the people, with your team with your key stakeholders. The best leaders are approachable, friendly and show sincere care for others. I don't think leaders who stay aloof in their offices have the best influence or effectiveness as leaders' Leadership is about being on the ground and knowing your people well. Every morning, I warmly welcomed and greeted the students and the parents at the school gate. I used to greet each child by their name as I could remember names of well over 300 students, this acknowledgement of each student as an individual from the leaders as mentioned by my teachers and parents played a massive role to boost the self-esteem of the students. First thing in the morning, playtime, lunchtime and home time, I religiously made it point to be present in the playground on time to engage with, meet, greet and say goodbye to the children – They were an extended family for me and my teachers named the 'The Swamily' School.

Apart from my official duties as headteacher, I used to put myself forward for play and lunchtime duties, most of the time, I was not required to do this but I made a point of being with the children. I engaged with the children by playing various sports. The time they scored a goal past me or bowled me out was like the kids winning a world cup match. At lunchtimes, I used to go in the kitchen and serve the children and the school community and eat thereafter. As much as we had a separate table in the dining hall for the teachers, I always made a point of eating with the children and I normally sat at the same table to get know the children personally in a different context), The virtue of humility dominates the character of a good head of a school. For him, children, parents and the school community members of whatever age group are human beings like himself and every person is unique. He is in a capacity to serve and his authority is never overtly mentioned.

Whenever staff needed time out to look after their immediate family members, or were not well themselves, as a leader I was always supportive and understanding. If a family member had passed away or was in hospital, I with one of my teachers always visited them. As much as I used to put the staff at the deep-end by assigning sometimes challenging tasks to them that I believed they were capable of, I allowed them to make mistakes. Every morning before school started, I used to visit members of staff to find out how they were getting along not only professionally but also personally as well. Any physical or mental health issues, I always was on hand to give them the support they needed. Knowing what was going on with staff and students was so important to me and that is why I always approached my role as headteacher with emotional intelligence, empathy and placed an emphasis on building strong relationships.

Bhatt: What have been some of your other key lessons and advice for other leaders?

Raja: Your primary job as leader is to create other leaders.

I learnt very early career that my main task as leaders is to create other leaders. Not all my teachers have had great leadership skills or other technical qualifications but this did not matter. When thinking about people who I wanted to help develop to become future leaders the key things for me that I would look out for was a positive attitude, lots of determination, passion and a desire to succeed. Knowledge and experience can be given to someone over time but it is very difficult to give someone passion, drive and the right attitude, to certain extent I believe those qualities are innate and leaders should look out for them especially when thinking about people they want to develop as future leaders.

Leaders should prioritise mental wellbeing.

Over the years of my career I have realised just how important the mental wellbeing of staff is. I think that this area is often overlooked but it is a major factor in the overall success of any organisation, how people feel at work and the things that are happening in their personal lives, impact performance. As a leader you have a responsibility to be supportive to your staff and look after them as much as you can. Valuing mental wellbeing is about creating a trusting environment where your staff are able to speak to you about things going on in their personal and professional life and the potential stress they may be under without being judged. When staff realise that leaders genuinely care for them, I think it leads to less turnover of staff and ultimately benefits the organisation as whole.

Leaders should strive to shape a positive culture.

Leaders massively impact the culture of an organisation and ultimately everyone is observing the leader. As a leader you should strive to create a culture of excellence but also allow people to make mistakes as that is an integral part of the learning and growth process. As a leader strive to be a good listener and also understand that your positive words of encouragement can work wonders, the value of genuine praise and appreciation should not be overlooked as leader, words have power and even more so when they come from the leader.

Hiten's case study of Mr Umesh Raja provides a real example of how true servant leaders behave in a business setting. Servant leadership is not a fad that is for the few but a way of behaving that can truly provide benefits to the people in the business and then have positive effects on the outcomes of the business. What leadership actions did you see in Hiten's case study that you could use?

Leadership in the real world

There are some incredible examples of great leadership and failures in leadership. We see these every day in person or in the news. Who do you think of as a great leader? Here are a few of the people I love to hear about their leadership approach. Let us start with the leadership approach of Jacinda Ardern, New Zealand Prime Minister. Jacinda needs little introduction and has been a breath of fresh air in world politics over the last 4 years as Prime Minister, and she was the world's youngest head of government at the age of thirty-seven. Vogue[18] identified many of Arden's successes as a leader, including her leadership in the aftermath of the Christchurch shootings in 2019. Her ability to bring together communities and her immediate imposition of tougher gun laws made headlines across the world. Whilst serving as Prime Minister, she took six weeks maternity leave following the arrival of Neve, her first child. She underlined her ability to lead her country whilst juggling the demands of a new-born when she attended United Nations by taking Neve with her to address the gathering.

New Zealand faced another disaster in 2019 as the volcano on White Island killing 16 people. Jacinda again led the disaster recovery with empathy. There are many other examples of her leadership which revolves around people and her efforts to listen to the voices of children. She has connected with people across the world and built an incredible profile as a leader which many other world leaders can aspire towards. My favourite quote from Jacinda is "To me, leadership is not about necessarily being the loudest in the room, but instead being the bridge, or the thing that is missing in the discussion and trying to build a consensus from there." Yet again, this is steeped in her willingness to guide and collaborate people.

In the business world I follow Dan Price, CEO of Gravity Payments (@DanPriceSeattle). I expect that many people will not know about Dan or his company and that is understandable. He is not anther Elon Musk. Instead, Dan is a CEO who gave up a million-dollar salary so he could increase the salaries for all his staff to $70,000. Every time I tell people about Dan, I get this barrage of negativity and questions around his motives. "He's only done it for the publicity Andy!" is something that I have been told repeatedly. Now, I agree that there are many leaders who may have done this and then the following year quietly doubled their salary or reduced the salary of new hires once the publicity had passed. Not Dan. He is vocal about big businesses and big bosses taking huge salaries whilst their workers suffer, and it is only possible to do what he is doing if you are leading from the front. Here is one of his tweets[19] calling out big business:

> *Min wage*
> *Costco: $16*
> *Walmart: $11*
>
> *Average pay*
> *Costco: $24*
> *Walmart: $15*
>
> *Employees on food stamps (subsidized by you)*
> *Costco: Virtually none*
> *Walmart: More than any other company*
>
> *Founder net worth*
> *Costco: not a billionaire*
> *Walmart: $220+ billion; up $30 billion in the pandemic*

His commitment to his push for a $70,000 minimum wage is revealed in his book, 'Worth It'. He describes the pain of growing his company and acquiring a new business, ChargeItPro, in his hometown of Boise, Idaho. The biggest challenge he faced was being able to move the employees to his minimum wage without compromising the future of the company. He set out on a journey to do this gradually but with a clear aim of parity across all employees. Dan continues to show brave leadership which is driven by his values and this can be witnessed every day on Twitter.

Another great leader to follow is James Timpson, CEO of Timpson's (@JamesTCobbler). James was awarded Business Leader of the Year at the 2019 Lloyds Bank National Business Awards and represents the third generation of Timpson's family leaders. James has helped drive the business forward by diversifying into many other markets from the same shops and the pods that now cover 500 sites around the UK. He has developed the 'Upside Down Management' ethos which is a culture based on kindness and trust. He believes strongly in this approach and if done correctly, colleagues will outperform against expectations. This approach is values-based as James strives to treat people equally. In fact, James has gone beyond the simple matter of talking about trust and actively recruits from prison leavers. Here is a tweet to support his recruitment campaign[20]:

> *Good news. Now our shops are all open we are recruiting again, so if you know of anyone with a criminal conviction, who has an amazing personality and is looking for work, please contact @darrenburns60 so we can sort an interview out.*

Just like Dan, this is not for publicity. James is a passionate believer in the recruitment of ex-offenders and Timpson's currently employ around 600. This accounts for 10% of their workforce and he continues to provide support as the Chair of the Prison Reform Trust. Here is a leader that believes in trust, and he has proved this throughout many years in business by hiring ex-offenders where many people would not. We need more leaders like James to provide the leadership role model for other business leaders and to inspire his own staff to become awesome leaders.

Leadership failure

Have you heard of Justin Kan? You may not have heard of Justin but you may have heard of Twitch, which he created and then sold in 2014 for $970m. In an era of people hiding failure or passing the blame, Justin announced on Twitter that his new company, Atrium, had failed and he had lost $75m in 36 months. (He had spent time and money completing legal paperwork for his start-up ventures and decided that Atrium could take away the pain of other entrepreneurs.)
He raised $10m of funding and assembled a great team with a vision and early adopters. He identified several factors in the downfall of Atrium. His ego kept on driving him to go bigger and they were not clear about their mission. The lack of goals caused issues with his co-founders, and they hired too fast which failed to deliver an aligned culture. Finally, he identified that they were trying to be everything to everyone. In his Twitter announcement, he said "My colleagues needed

to be supported and set up for success. My "win or die" strategy didn't work and worse, strained relationships." The final straw was realising that he had no passion for Legal technology.

This is such a refreshing post on Twitter. Amongst the junk that often fills my Twitter feed, this was a fantastic read. How many more people could write posts like this to let others know that success is not instant and needs more than one attempt? Here are some more examples of leadership failure taken from the outcomes of Employment Tribunals. I am an avid reader of these updates as they give summaries of genuine cases where people have suffered often through the failures of their leaders.

- Rawnsley v QAS – After a disagreement with his manager about cleaning a work area, the Managing Director punched Rawnsley, pushed him and told him to leave the premises. The MD later sent Rawnsley a text: "Jake, this is Tony. Apologies for my half in our incident. It is my intention to pay you for today and tomorrow and you can resume work Monday. I will assume if I do not hear from you, and you do not show Monday you have decided to move on. I will need a change in attitude from you and I am willing to work with you on this. This is called a cooling off period". Rawnsley did not return to work and succeeded with a claim at the Employment Tribunal for a breach of the implied term of trust and confidence.

- Tuchkova v Artemev - A Russian qualified lawyer was employed as a Legal Project Manager before proceeding on maternity leave. A month before her expected return to work, Ms Tuchkova attended a discussion with her manager where he advised her there was "no work" anymore and that she should find another job. When asked why he had not raised this with her earlier, he responded "... it was important that he should leave her undisturbed while she was breastfeeding as he was concerned that the shock of a prospective redundancy might affect her ability to feed her child and that the child was more important than the mother." The Employment Tribunal found that Ms Tuchkova had been unfairly dismissed.

Some other failings from big business also give an insight into how wrong leaders can be.

WeWork publicly filed its IPO (Initial Public Offering) paperwork on 14th August 2019. That was the start of the problems for its leader and cofounder Adam Neumann. The filing brought about previously undisclosed facts about WeWork's structure and governance. The amount of stock owned by Neumann, coupled with x10 voting rights than a standard shareholder was also a source of contention. Added to that, the personal loans he received from WeWork, the money he had to pay back with an amended IPO filing and questions about the lack of female representation on the board, Neumann gave up his seat on the board to remove the 'distraction' from the difficulties they were facing. In 2019, just six weeks had passed between the IPO filing and Neumann's departure. In that time, WeWork had started to close offices, and by November 2019 they had made 2400 people redundant.

Luckin may not be a brand familiar to you, but at their zenith, they were a bigger coffee house than Starbucks across China. In 2019, they were valued at $4.2bn and in 2020 had 4,500 restaurants compared to Starbucks'4,300. By early 2020, Luckin were under the magnifying glass of Muddy Waters, a US based short-selling business, who had alleged they had invented sales of over $300m. After admitting this inflated income, Luckin's success faltered as they were delisted from the stock exchange, paid a settlement of $180m to the US Stock Exchange Commission and overhauled their leadership team who had overseen the fabricated finances.

Turning to the fast-food business, former CEO, Steve Easterbrook, was dismissed from McDonalds after admitting a relationship with another employee. But as Easterbrook and McDonalds parted company, more information became known which resulted in a deeper investigation by McDonald's. It was alleged that Easterbrook had relationships with three other McDonald's employees and had used his corporate email to exchange explicit pictures and videos. They also discovered that he had given stock grants to some women for thousands of dollars which was not clear at the time of his departure. As Eastbrook had allegedly tried to hide his tracks by deleting evidence from his devices, McDonalds sought to recoup the settlement they had made with Easterbrook. The case is yet to be resolved (2021) although Easterbrook claimed that McDonalds knew about the relationships and the stock options when the settlement was made.

You may be familiar with the next case centred around Nissan, but I have included it here to explain more detail around their former CEO, Carlos Goshn. He had arrived at Nissan as a renowned leader in the automotive industry, quickly winning a variety of awards including Asia Businessman of the Year. He held a raft of positions as both CEO and Chairman of a strategic alliance including Nissan, Renault and Mitsubishi. He stepped down from his role as CEO of Nissan in April 2017 but by November 2018, he was arrested and charged with under-reporting his salary and misuse of company assets.

The case focussed on his undeclared earnings from 2011-2015 where he declared only half of his $88m earnings. 2019 saw further charges made for misappropriation of funds from Nissan whilst Renault discovered €11m of expenses which needed further explanation. Whilst under house arrest in Japan, Goshn fled the country to evade justice in an escape plot normally reserved for a blockbuster film.

For any Volkswagen owners, you will be aware that in September 2015, Volkswagen were embroiled in the emissions cheating scandal that exposed how they had institutionally set out to defraud governments and customers about the true level of emissions from their vehicles. CEO Martin Winterkorn dismissed any knowledge of these actions but resigned shortly after his vehicles were found to have cheated the US emission test. After Winterkorn's departure, Bernd Osterloh, from the VW board, wrote "We need, in the future, a climate in which problems are not hidden. Rather, problems should be openly communicated to superiors....we need a culture in which it is possible and permissible to argue with your superior about the best way to go."

The leadership failures highlighted here cover many topics: physical violence, sexual discrimination, unethical decision making, greed, financial mismanagement and misconduct. There are many more examples that could be citied but the message here is that leadership failures can happen in all businesses. We may expect that global businesses should be better able to prevent leaders from committing acts that endanger the future of their business or that small local businesses may be more aware of the needs of the few employees they have. This is not the case. Leadership failures are commonplace. They happen in all businesses and it takes substantial efforts to identify and expose these failings. Justin Kan's candidness is not normal and we should enjoy the learning that we can all benefit from whilst encouraging leaders around us to be more open.

Leadership role models

For the last 18 months, I have had the pleasure of running a podcast called Leadership, the future and tea, speaking with many business leaders, authors, academics and coaches. These discussions helped me to reflect on my own leadership approach and what the future held for leaders and different industries. I want to share with you some of the amazing thoughts from our guests.

The most powerful question I asked during these episodes was 'Who is your leadership role model?'. It is a question I have often tried to answer for myself on many occasions. Each time, I come back to some key people in my life: parents and Scout leaders. My parents taught me about integrity, working with people and the need to have a balance in life. My dad would often say 'Work hard and enjoy yourself'.

The message was clear but as a teenager I didn't really get the leadership message that was hidden in these few words. When I talked to him about this, he explained that he was referring to leading my own wellness and that of others, and that without a balanced approach to life, you are not as productive as you could be. Equally as important to me is my experience in the Scouts. I had the pleasure of meeting some incredible people who gave their time freely to share knowledge, skills and build my confidence that I would carry to every job I ever had. These Scout leaders were unsung heroes, and it took me a long time to realise that I learnt so much from their leadership skills as they motivated, inspired, mentored and showed trust in so many young people.

Whilst you ponder your own answer to the question 'Who is your leadership role model?', here are the responses from a selection of our guests:

Lori Niles-Hofmann, Senior Learning EdTech Transformation Strategist and blogger on lori.ca.

> *"The role model that I really, really appreciated, is a gentleman by the name of Steve Woods, who was the Chief Technology Officer for Eloqua. He grew that from a start-up, him and his business partner Paul Teshima, they grew this into from a start-up all the way up into being IPO and then being bought by Oracle for a billion. It was an incredible story. And why I consider him the model of leadership and still do, he took the moment to connect with every single person who came along that journey. If you saw him, you would never know that he was the CTO of this massive organisation. He had this presence and this way of speaking, and he wasn't afraid to get us roll up his sleeves and just get coding because he loved it. I loved that, that passion in him and that ability to straddle all layers and to do it with grace and dignity. One story about him that I remember is when they went for IPO, he went down onto the call centre floor and he wrote a personal check as an interest free loan for anyone who could not afford to buy in. Really, and I just think Wow, that's amazing because he realised to somebody who's you maybe at the time earning $40k, this was a barrier to entry. And he's like, no, you're part of this journey. That was a huge amount of respect for him."*

Amy Jen Su, Co-founder/Managing Partner of Parvis Partners and author of 'The Leader You Want to Be'.

> *"When I think about that, who I most aspire to be like, the person that comes to mind is my 75-year-old mother.*
>
> *And she reminds me of an adage that a CEO, once shared with me, which was, leadership isn't a title. It's about who you are, the decisions you make, the actions you take, the impact you have on others. And truthfully, my mom was a day-care teacher. For most of her career, she took care of two-year old kids, so not an easy job. When I reflect on the impact she had on those kids on her classroom on our family, she did a lot of volunteer*

work in her later stage of life after she retired. She's a breast cancer survivor. She's just an incredibly resilient, tough woman who's kind and always taught us and I observed her always trying to do the right thing. If you think of Jim Collins, his article, Level Five Leadership and a Level Five Leader, where a leader exemplifies the paradox of iron will and great humility. I think that's the perfect way of describing my mom and who I try to be in the world as well."

Mark Samlal, CEO and Founder of PayGroup Ltd.

"My leadership role model would no doubt be one of PayGroup's shareholders, and prominent Australian businessmen, Mr. Philip Cove. Philip was instrumental in assisting myself with a group of others to really do a massive turnaround in the payroll and HR space in the late 1990s. I was involved in that in a sales leadership capacity, and the expansion and to get into Asia and my experience to come to Asia was really formulated. So Mr. Phil Cave, if you're listening, I hope you will be. Thank you very much. So, you've been a great mentor and business advocate and supporter of mine for over 20 years now."

Deke Copenhaver, former Mayor of Augusta and author of 'Change Maker'.

"My father is really true north. He grew up one of five children raised by a single mother during the Great Depression. He flew B17 bombers in World War Two. Went on to climb the ladder and become a corporate CEO, but never let us forget where we came from. He never saw himself above the people that work with him.

After he passed, people said he would come and walk the floor of the factory and speak to the rank-and-file employees. So, he really was my true north and I think he lost his father when he was 12 years old. So, I think his military service really instilled in him the principles of duty, honour and integrity. So, my father was in his early 40s when I was born, but to be raised by somebody from the greatest generation, he truly is my leadership model."

Beth Armknecht Miller, Leadership Development Advisor, Executive Coach and author of 'Replaceable'.

"I would actually probably say my mother. She had to lead for four kids under the age of five. And she did it with grace and dignity and an empathy. And, you know, she was just a great role model for me growing up."

Mark Schaefer, Keynote speaker, Marketing Consultant and author of 'Marketing Rebellion'.

> *"That's an easy one to answer. One of my great heroes was the great American author and consultant Peter Drucker. I got to study under Professor Drucker for three years at the Claremont Graduate University, when I was getting my MBA, and that was really a life changing experience. There's not a week that goes by that I don't hear his voice in my head. He has that kind of an impact on people. And I'll add he was a very kind man as well. There was nothing ostentatious about him whatsoever. He was like a grandfather. He was just very accessible and very kind. I think the biggest lesson that that Dr. Drucker taught me, and it was hard to escape this lesson, if you were ever around him was this idea of humility.*
>
> *And he would get very, very angry. It was a very competitive programme to even get into. I was actually the youngest person ever admitted to the programme. So, most of the people in this programme were Vice Presidents. They know everything, and he would teach by the case study method. And so, we would dissect these problems then, of course, the natural instinct of these experienced leaders was to solve the problem, and he would get so angry.*
>
> *And he would say, what makes you believe that you're so gifted? How can you be so arrogant that these people who have been working in this company for 30 years, they can't figure out the problem? But you can. Your role is not to have all the right answers but is to ask the right questions. They're missing the questions. That's your goal. If they can just ask the right question. They'll get to the answer. And that's what your role is, as a leader. You don't have to know everything. You don't have to have every answer, but you've got to ask the right questions."*

Yetunde Hofmann, Non-Executive Director, Founder of Solaris, Change Adviser and author of 'Beyond Engagement'.

> *"It took me quite a while to think about this because there's so many different traits. And so, then I landed on one person, my leadership role model of all time is Jesus Christ.*
> *And why would I say Jesus Christ? Because he's the perfection of servant leadership. He is about inclusion and diversity. He accepts you for who you are. His authentic selfless when you read about what Jesus did and who he is, and he's empowering him out the disciples, and he empowered us."*

Between our podcast guests, they identified some incredible role models including parents, religious leaders, academics and business leaders.

During our life, we meet a multitude of people and takeaway some piece of learning from many more that we remember. Asking people to identify their leadership role model is a great question for any interview, especially where it is a leadership role you are recruiting for.

How can I adopt the correct leadership approach?

As can be seen in the examples I have provided in this chapter, each leader has crafted their own leadership approach. The successful people, and we are going to focus on these leaders, have often done this through a set of values that they have then translated into their work. Dan Price's stoic belief that people should be paid a fair wage stems from his upbringing and beliefs. James Timpson is driven to help ex-offenders and can see the potential in people. His approach is based on trust. Jacinda wants to focus on the people and communicate openly with as many as possible, both young and old.

Not all these approaches will be correct for you. To help you discover your approach, complete the following questions:

Figure 3.1 – Discovery questions

Focus	Question
Integrity	Do you readily admit to your mistakes?
	Do you support people to achieve their ambitions even though it will cause you extra work or loss of an employee?
	How would you act if you discovered someone stealing or defrauding your business?
	Would you stop unethical practice even if it meant losing business?
Self	What makes you angry or upset?
	What frustrates you at work?
	What gives you an incredible sense of achievement?
	What was your best day at work and why?
	What is important to you? (money, title, helping others, promotion, house, car)
	What do you worry about?

	Who inspires you and why?
	What are you passionate about?
	How do you learn and grow?
People	How do you support the growth of others?
	When did you last help someone without an expected return?
	How do you react when targets are missed by your team?
	How good are you at giving feedback?
	How transparent are you with your communications?
Impact	Do you deliver what you commit to?
	Do you achieve challenging targets and set targets for others?
	What do you want to be known for?
	What is your personal brand?
	What will your legacy be when you leave your current job?

The answers to these questions will not directly show the leadership approach you should take or pigeonhole you into a named approach. What they will give you is an opportunity to reflect on what you believe about yourself. Now for the difficult part. Hand the list of questions to some colleagues, friends and family and ask them to provide their assessment of you. There will be a difference between your answers and their answers.

- Integrity – This is your core. As a leader, your integrity is key to survival and success. Your reflections and the observations from your trusted friends/colleagues should be exceptional. If not, spend time considering how you can make immediate improvements and, what you need to do about decisions you may need to unpick.

- Self – This area will help you uncover your purpose and what is important to you. A great leader will have a clear purpose and be driven towards it. An average leader will try to drive at many ideas and goals but never really achieve any. The powerful outcomes of this sections are the items that don't help you drive towards your purpose and therefore, you should stop doing.

- People – Your leadership of those around you is the most important part of your job. The feedback and reflection you identify here will help you to become a better leader if you act upon the feedback provided.

- Impact – As a leader, you will be judged more on your results than ever before. Your targets will be more impactful and wide-ranging. Throughout your journey, you will build a personal brand that will remain in the stories and culture of the business after you have left. This is your opportunity to ensure that corporate stories that are told about you in the future are inspiring to the next generation of leaders.

These items combined represent your leadership approach. You may wish to amend the list to accommodate your local context but the four areas of Integrity, Self, People and Impact remain the four central pillars of your leadership approach.

Summary

There is no one correct way to lead. Personally, I aspire to be more of a servant leader and create an environment in which my team can perform to their best whilst I provide the resources they need. But that may not be right for you. Every leader needs to have a passion for their people to be successful. Coupled with a clear vision and effective communication, you then are in control of the leadership approach you take. Each leader will form their own unique approach but you can use the discovery questions in covering integrity, self, people and impact to understand more about your own leadership approach. Once you have completed this self-review, you need to reflect and then plan how you will adapt your leadership approach in the future.

Reflective activities

- Who are the real leaders in your business?

- Do you know how your approach of leadership is perceived?

- Are you a Servant Leader?

- Who are your leadership role models and what can you take from their example into your own leadership?

- What leadership failures and leadership successes are you aware of in your business? What can you learn from them?

Suggested reading

- Su A J. (2019). *The leader you want to be*. Harvard Business Review Press. Boston.
- Ashton J. (2021). *The nine types of leader*. Kogan Page. London
- Greenleaf (1977). *Servant Leadership* [25th Anniversary Edition]: *A Journey into the Nature of Legitimate Power and Greatness*. Paulist Press. New York.

Chapter 4

Communication

"Write to be understood, speak to be heard, read to grow."
Lawrence Clark Powell (Author)

Introduction

Effective communication is the way that great leaders stand out from ordinary leaders. Great leaders are strong orators and writers but they always have a standout preference. What you can't afford to do as a leader is be fantastic at speaking and poor at writing or vice versa. You must have a high baseline on both.

A leader's communication is the first skill that is judged. So, it's critical. For leaders and aspiring leaders in all diverse levels of the organisation, one of the main factors that can make them stand out is their communication. Whether it's right, wrong or it's taken out of context, that leader owns the success of that piece of communication. The important part about the communication is the effect on morale, the productivity and the financial results that then follow. We will look at several aspects of communication in this chapter and you can apply those three measures (morale, productivity and financial results) against most of them.

Communication within a business happens at the macro level, micro level and all levels in between.

Figure 4.1 – Communication continuum

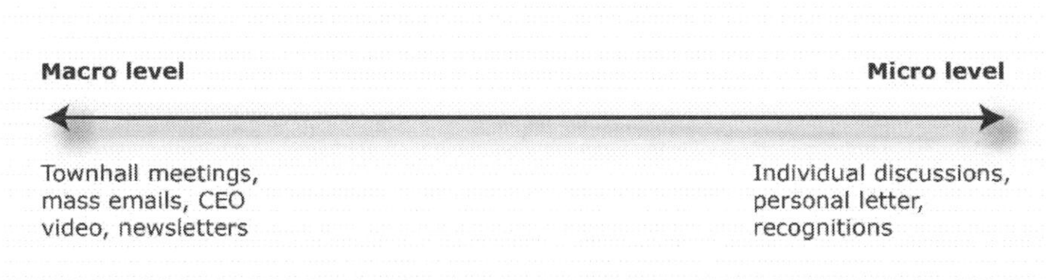

Social media has brought a new communication skill that is required and it is very different than the 'traditional' channels that many leaders will have perfected over the years. It has a wide reach, immediate and cannot be undone as many leaders have discovered to their cost.

Rounded leaders need to be skilled at all aspects of communication and this is just one element. Additionally, in an increasingly connected world, social media as a form of communication both internally and externally, cannot be ignored. I will touch more on the impact of social media in the Networks chapter.

Communication as a tool for gaining support and establishing credibility

A classic mistake for leaders in all environments is to communicate without first understanding the context in which they are working. Politicians are great at responding to a question they know nothing about but giving an answer that means nothing. At that point, they have lost credibility and made any future communications more difficult with people who they need to influence. Covey's '*7 Habits of Highly Effective People*'[21] contains a great piece of advice as the 5th habit. "Seek first to understand, then to be understood." This means that until you have understood the context and culture, don't rush in to communicate. The understanding part will take longer than the communicating part but it will make the communication more impactful when you do communicate.

There are some amazing examples where leaders have failed with the communications and these mistakes include a lack of understanding, lack of empathy or just poor timing. It's incredible that leaders of multi-national companies can make such mistakes when they have access to the brightest talent around to help craft every message. Mediocre communications or poorly timed communications can have an immediate effect for the people involved. But for the leader delivering the message, the effect is broken trust and a lack of credibility. Here are some examples of poor communication from business showing how wrong you can get it.

At AOL, the CEO Tim Armstrong was addressing 1000 employees of Patch at a townhall to discuss the future of the business. Patch was a business created by Armstong and aimed at satisfying a market for local information, news and updates at carefully selected target audiences. The business model was undermined after Patch had started to open sites that weren't favoured by marketers and subsequently, this led to the downsizing of Patch. During the townhall convened to address this, Armstrong gave many strong messages to the employees. Including, that if they did not agree with what he was telling them or they weren't committed to the platform they should simply leave.
The tone of delivery wasn't great but it got worse. Abel Lenz, Creative Director, was taking photos of the event when Armstrong publicly fired him. He simply said "Abel put that camera down right now. Abel. You're fired. Out." What followed was uproar and an email from Armstrong to explain his actions and the further context behind his quick decision. It was too late. The publicity around the firing was merely the

start of Patch's problems which led to a sale and the redundancy of 300 people. Although not all due to this communication issue, Forbes[22] identified that AOL had lost around $200M on Patch but that could be as high as $300M.

The Deepwater Horizon oil spill on 20 April 2010, lasted for 87 days releasing 4.9M barrels of oil into the Gulf of Mexico. This started with an explosion, which all but destroyed the rig, and is thought to have killed 11 workers, although their bodies have never been found. Whilst the ecological disaster was raging out of control and the loss of life was frantically being investigated, BP CEO Tony Hayward appeared on a news bulletin and said "I'm sorry. We're sorry for the massive disruption it's caused their lives. There's no one who wants this over more than I do. I'd like my life back."

Although he was trying to say that he wants to see an end to the disaster for all those people who were affected, it came across as a selfish statement about the impact on himself. In July 2010, Hayward announced his resignation from BP but this was following several other communications gaffes after the disaster. Businesses who rely on CEOs and other leaders to front media events need to ensure they are trained and ready to deliver a credible statement. This was an avoidable communication failure.

For the final example of poor communications, here is a disaster from a Public Relations business in Scotland. Beattie Communications Chair & founder, Gordon Beattie, published a post on LinkedIn in February 2021 which cropped up in my LinkedIn feed. I was astonished when I read it as it contained "At Beattie Communications we don't hire blacks, gays or Catholics." The post went on to explain that they only hire talented people but by then the damage was done.

A few days later, after posting a detailed apology, he stepped down from his position as Chair so the "agency can look to the future". Even the professionals who are hired to avoid such errors can make devasting communication blunders!

Some of the greatest learning you can access is when leaders around you get it wrong. These examples should give you the chance to look at how other leaders have failed so you can reflect on what you would do differently. Once you've done that, there are some examples below which show some excellent communication.

Examples of great communication

I put significant importance on the new leader's first business-wide communication. It sets the scene for the months that follow. It also allows the new leader to show some of their personal life and connect with individuals in a way that would normally take years of small talk.

Years ago, I never took the time to do this and simply got stuck in from the first day in my new job. But I witnessed some great leaders taking the time to plan their arrival in a new job, how they would initially communicate to everyone and also considering who they needed to quickly build relationships with, both internally and externally.

To help understand this better, I've included some examples of arrival communications from different leaders so you can see their approach, including their openness, as they introduced themselves to everyone. I've used examples from well-known businesses but don't be fooled into thinking this is an activity for multi-national companies. These communications are for everyone as the impact lasts for the tenure of the leader.

Satya Nadella was installed as the new CEO of Microsoft on 4 February 2014 after arriving at Microsoft in 1992. Satya was only the third CEO in the history of Microsoft and followed the footsteps of Bill Gates and Steve Ballmer. He took control of Microsoft when it was seen as a declining presence amongst the new heavyweight tech giants and that the culture needed an overhaul. A fantastic opportunity for a new leader or a daunting task? Here is his email which he sent to all employees on his first day in office.

> *Today is a very humbling day for me. It reminds me of my very first day at Microsoft, 22 years ago. Like you, I had a choice about where to come to work. I came here because I believed Microsoft was the best company in the world. I saw then how clearly we empower people to do magical things with our creations and ultimately make the world a better place. I knew there was no better company to join if I wanted to make a difference. This is the very same inspiration that continues to drive me today.*
>
> *It is an incredible honor for me to lead and serve this great company of ours. Steve and Bill have taken it from an idea to one of the greatest and most universally admired companies in the world. I've been fortunate to work closely with both Bill and Steve in my different roles at Microsoft, and as I step in as CEO, I've asked Bill to devote additional time to the company, focused on technology and products. I'm also looking forward to working with John Thompson as our new Chairman of the Board.*
>
> *While we have seen great success, we are hungry to do more. Our industry does not respect tradition — it only respects innovation. This is a critical time for the industry and for Microsoft. Make no mistake, we are headed for greater places — as technology evolves and we evolve with and ahead of it. Our job is to ensure that Microsoft thrives in a mobile and cloud-first world.*

As we start a new phase of our journey together, I wanted to share some background on myself and what inspires and motivates me.

Who am I?

I am 46. I've been married for 22 years and we have 3 kids. And like anyone else, a lot of what I do and how I think has been shaped by my family and my overall life experiences. Many who know me say I am also defined by my curiosity and thirst for learning. I buy more books than I can finish. I sign up for more online courses than I can complete. I fundamentally believe that if you are not learning new things, you stop doing great and useful things. So family, curiosity and hunger for knowledge all define me.

Why am I here?

I am here for the same reason I think most people join Microsoft — to change the world through technology that empowers people to do amazing things. I know it can sound hyperbolic — and yet it's true. We have done it, we're doing it today, and we are the team that will do it again.

I believe over the next decade computing will become even more ubiquitous and intelligence will become ambient. The coevolution of software and new hardware form factors will intermediate and digitize — many of the things we do and experience in business, life and our world. This will be made possible by an ever-growing network of connected devices, incredible computing capacity from the cloud, insights from big data, and intelligence from machine learning.

This is a software-powered world.

It will better connect us to our friends and families and help us see, express, and share our world in ways never before possible. It will enable businesses to engage customers in more meaningful ways.

I am here because we have unparalleled capability to make an impact.

Why are we here?

In our early history, our mission was about the PC on every desk and home, a goal we have mostly achieved in the developed world. Today we're focused on a broader range of devices. While the deal is not yet complete, we will welcome to our family Nokia devices and services and the new mobile capabilities they bring us.

As we look forward, we must zero in on what Microsoft can uniquely contribute to the world. The opportunity ahead will require us to reimagine a lot of what we have done in the past for a mobile and cloud-first world, and do new things.

We are the only ones who can harness the power of software and deliver it through devices and services that truly empower every individual and every organization. We are the only company with history and continued focus in building platforms and ecosystems that create broad opportunity.

Qi Lu captured it well in a recent meeting when he said that Microsoft uniquely empowers people to "do more." This doesn't mean that we need to do more things, but that the work we do empowers the world to do more of what they care about — get stuff done, have fun, communicate and accomplish great things. This is the core of who we are, and driving this core value in all that we do — be it the cloud or device experiences — is why we are here.

What do we do next?

To paraphrase a quote from Oscar Wilde — we need to believe in the impossible and remove the improbable.

This starts with clarity of purpose and sense of mission that will lead us to imagine the impossible and deliver it. We need to prioritize innovation that is centered on our core value of empowering users and organizations to "do more." We have picked a set of high-value activities as part of our One Microsoft strategy. And with every service and device launch going forward we need to bring more innovation to bear around these scenarios.

Next, every one of us needs to do our best work, lead and help drive cultural change. We sometimes underestimate what we each can do to make things happen and overestimate what others need to do to move us forward. We must change this.

Finally, I truly believe that each of us must find meaning in our work. The best work happens when you know that it's not just work, but something that will improve other people's lives. This is the opportunity that drives each of us at this company.

Many companies aspire to change the world. But very few have all the elements required: talent, resources, and perseverance. Microsoft has proven that it has all three in abundance. And as the new CEO, I can't ask for a better foundation.

Let's build on this foundation together.

Satya

The next example of an arrival email is from Chris Kempczinski, CEO McDonald's, and was sent to his employees in November 2019. Chris had arrived following the demise of Steve Easterbrook after allegations that he had violated corporate policies and entered into a relationship with one of his employees. Just as Satya Nadella faced some challenges upon his arrival, Chris' challenges were more about the credibility and integrity of the CEO. Here's his email to all McDonald's employees:

SUBJECT: Our Path Forward Together

I am excited to take the reins of this incredible company and grateful for the Board's confidence in me. I am particularly fortunate to be surrounded by such a talented team as we take this brand into the future.

I have been a lifelong fan of McDonald's. Like so many of our customers, some of my fondest childhood memories were of my experiences at a McDonald's. Since joining the company in 2015, I've been able to see up-close how all three legs of the stool work together in an incredible partnership to bring our brand to life in the restaurants and communities that we serve.

I'm happiest when I'm in our restaurants, visiting with franchisees, their crew and our customers. Listening to their stories, I'm reminded about the larger purpose that our brand plays in the lives of millions of people around the world. Yes, we serve delicious food and offer great experiences, but our brand means so much more. We stand for opportunity and empowerment for everyone. McDonald's is a special company, and it's my privilege to work with all of you to make a difference in the lives of so many.

When I joined McDonald's to lead global strategy, business development and innovation, we were in the midst of a critical turnaround. Developing a strategic plan was central to harnessing the power and relevance of the brand for our business and customers. We decided to refocus on the customer and met with almost 10,000 of our guests around the world to understand their needs and learn how we could better serve them. This "global listening tour" was the inspiration for our Velocity Growth Plan, and the success we've enjoyed ever since is a powerful reminder to always keep our focus on the customer. I expect that we will continue to use the Velocity Growth Plan as our strategic roadmap, as the retain/regain/convert framework is still highly relevant to the opportunities available to us.

I also want to thank Steve for his many contributions. Steve brought me into McDonald's and he was a patient and helpful mentor. I wish him all the best in his future endeavors.

McDonald's has a deep bench of talent and, as one of my first moves as CEO, I'm excited to announce Joe Erlinger as President, McDonald's USA. Joe and I have worked closely together since I first joined the Company. He is a respected leader who is returning to the U.S. after working around the world for McDonald's, most recently as President, International Operated Markets. He has a proven track record of driving strong results through collaboration with franchisees and a relentless focus on the customer. I am confident in all Joe will bring to the U.S. business. We're also working to identify Joe's successor.

Thank you for your commitment to McDonald's and for all you do every day, across more than 100 markets, to drive us forward and help us reach our incredible potential.

Chris Kempczinski

The reasons for the arrival of Satya and Chris were very different but both mentioned their predecessors and recognised their achievements. No animosity. Just a mention that thanked them for what they did and then moving onto their other messages. This helps write them into the company's history and ensure that their supporters are not alienated from the incoming CEO.
At a time of change, and in Chris' case, corporate turbulence, the need to transition smoothly into the new regime is critical. Another point you may have noticed is the frequency that both use the word 'we'. Satya is more prolific using 'we' but the outcome is that people are brought together and focused on the future they are trying to create. Although both are notable examples of communication, my preference is for Satya's approach to sharing information about himself, his family and his interests shows his openness from the start. Next time you commence a new role, think about your arrival communication and what you will say to your new team and how this will set the foundation for your success.

Additionally, there is a lot to be learnt from the way leaders leave a business and the communication that surrounds their departure. You should not burn bridges when leaving a business – even if the choice to leave wasn't yours. Too often, poor leaders will want to 'grandstand' their leaving with comments or actions that serve no purpose. If you are leaving, it's too late to make a noise other than it may help to settle your bruised ego. At this point, the business is already looking forward to your successor! The real measure of a leader is to leave on good terms and know that the world is too small to make pockets of 'no return'. In the future, either party may wish to come back to the table to discuss business or you may want to access the talented people in your former business. To be successful in securing either the people or the business, both are dependent on the way you departed the business. Here are some examples of leaving messages from leaders that serve to underline what a final communication to everyone can look like.

David Kar, former CEO of Tumblr[23], wrote his farewell message to his team in November 2017. This is full of appreciation, awareness of the journey they have all been on together and encouraging about the future.

> *Friends and colleagues*
>
> *After nearly 11 years, I've decided that 2017 will be my last year at Tumblr.*
>
> *It is truly overwhelming to write those words. But I have the comfort of knowing I leave Tumblr in better hands that my own. Jeff is the most capable and caring leader I've ever met, which I say with no exaggeration. Simon has worked tirelessly to support us and everything that makes Tumblr special. But even more, they are both true believers in what we've built and how much we can still do.*
>
> *I look back with so much pride. At a generation of artists, writers, creators, and crusaders that have redefined our culture, and who we have helped to empower.*
>
> *There are no words, though, that can express how sincerely grateful I am for the privilege of working with you. This team and place has been my family and home for most of my adult life. That I gotten to spend this time working with people so spectacularly talented and unstoppably optimistic is a blessing and I hope you have shared, and will continue to share.*
>
> *I beg you to understand that my decision comes after months of reflection on my personal ambitions, and at no cost to my hopefulness for Tumblr's future or the impact I know it can have. The internet is at a crossroads of which this team can play a fundamental role in shaping. You are in the driver seat, and I am so excited to see where you go!*

Thank you for allowing me this honor.

David

Former UBS CEO, Andrea Orcel[24], sent this email September 2018 as he prepared to join Santander as their new CEO and Banco Santander.

Subject: Onward

By now, you will have heard that I will be leaving UBS Investment Bank in October to take up a new position as CEO of Santander Group. There will be plenty of time for goodbyes so let me use this moment simply to say thank you.

Thank you for the immense honor of serving this business and this exceptional team for the past seven years.

We have achieved some incredible things in that time and succeeded in ways that many thought would not be possible. Through the Accelerate program we shifted from a business that was unfocused and lagging, absorbing too much cost while destroying value, to one that is focused and strengthened, using less capital and creating value. We stopped trying to be the biggest investment bank and focused on being the best.

Thank you for your dedication, your intensity and your commitment to our vision that has transformed us into a winning team.

Because of you we outperformed throughout the cycle. We delivered best-in-class returns ahead of both European and US peers. We went from number seven in Research, to number one in the world. We built a culture that allowed colleagues to stand tall and be proud of the work we were doing.

And thank you for taking ownership of the future. I said at this year's Partnership Summits that if we each take ownership, as individuals and as teams, then the sky's the limit. This business has a unique opportunity to benefit from the disruption of digital. With an organization that is stable, highly profitable, built on a culture of innovation, you have all the ingredients you need to win. It is in your hands now.

I am delighted that Piero and Rob will now lead this team as co-Presidents. They will serve, as they have done in their current roles, with great distinction and I wish them well – and good luck!

Life is a series of hellos and goodbyes, but still this moment is bittersweet. I truly love this business and it has been a tremendous experience working for – and with – Sergio. Believe me when I tell you that I wouldn't have left for anything less than a client I've been advising and working with for my whole career.

In the immortal words of Winnie the Pooh: "How lucky I am to have something that makes saying goodbye so hard."

Onward,

Andrea

(Side note: Following such a great email, Andrea arrived at Santander but was soon engulfed in a contractual argument between UBS, Santander and the European regulators. Andrea was released from his contract in July 2019 and commenced a €100M lawsuit against Santander for breach of contract.)

Marissa Meyer[25], former Yahoo CEO, sent this email to all Yahoo employees in June 2017 as she was leaving to set up Sunshine with a former colleague.

323 days ago, we announced that Verizon would be acquiring Yahoo's operating business. Today, I can announce that the transaction has officially closed. While reaching this moment has certainly been a long road traveled, it marks the end of an era for Yahoo, as well as the beginning of a new chapter – it's an emotional time for all of us. Given the inherent changes to my role, I'll be leaving the company. However, I want all of you to know that I'm brimming with nostalgia, gratitude, and optimism.

It's been my great honor and privilege to be a part of this team for the last 5 years. Together, we have rebuilt, reinvented, strengthened, and modernized our products, our business, and our company.

Looking back on my time at Yahoo, we have confronted seemingly insurmountable business challenges, along with many surprise twists and turns. I've seen our teams navigate these hurdles and mountains in ways that have not only made Yahoo a better company, but also made all of us far stronger. During these past 5 years, we've built products that delight our users, focused on our clients' businesses, driven substantial value for our shareholders, and endeavored to make Yahoo the absolute best place to work. I want to take a moment to remind you of some of our many achievements together. They are remarkable, and we should all be very proud.

As I look back on these achievements, I want to sincerely thank every single Yahoo employee, past and present, for your contributions both large and small. I'm tremendously grateful for all of the hard work and the many sacrifices you've made. We always endeavored to do the right thing for our users, advertisers, shareholders, and fellow Yahoos. This has required the most impressive displays of teamwork, innovation, and resilience I've ever seen, and working with you has made my time as CEO nothing short of a privilege.

Finally, I want to thank our founders, Filo and Jerry. Every entrepreneur's wildest dream is to change the world with their ideas, and you've done just that. From day one, your tenacity and whimsy helped create one of the most special companies of all time – one that has employed more than 175,000 people, generated over $77B in revenue, and has informed, connected, and entertained a large portion of humanity. You've inspired all of us with your brilliance, values, and passion, and I will forever be in awe of you and I will forever be your biggest fan :-)

Yaho-o-oo!

Marissa

In the final example, Jeff Bezos[26], founder and former CEO of Amazon, sent this email to all his 'fellow Amazonians' in February 2021.

Fellow Amazonians:

I'm excited to announce that this Q3 I'll transition to Executive Chair of the Amazon Board and Andy Jassy will become CEO. In the Exec Chair role, I intend to focus my energies and attention on new products and early initiatives. Andy is well known inside the company and has been at Amazon almost as long as I have. He will be an outstanding leader, and he has my full confidence.

This journey began some 27 years ago. Amazon was only an idea, and it had no name. The question I was asked most frequently at that time was, "What's the internet?" Blessedly, I haven't had to explain that in a long while.

Today, we employ 1.3 million talented, dedicated people, serve hundreds of millions of customers and businesses, and are widely recognized as one of the most successful companies in the world.

How did that happen? Invention. Invention is the root of our success. We've done crazy things together, and then made them normal. We pioneered customer reviews, 1-Click, personalized recommendations, Prime's insanely-fast shipping, Just Walk Out shopping, the Climate Pledge, Kindle, Alexa, marketplace, infrastructure cloud computing, Career Choice, and much more. If you get it right, a few years after a surprising invention, the new thing has become normal. People yawn. And that yawn is the greatest compliment an inventor can receive.

I don't know of another company with an invention track record as good as Amazon's, and I believe we are at our most inventive right now. I hope you are as proud of our inventiveness as I am. I think you should be.

As Amazon became large, we decided to use our scale and scope to lead on important social issues. Two high-impact examples: our $15 minimum wage and the Climate Pledge. In both cases, we staked out leadership positions and then asked others to come along with us. In both cases, it's working. Other large companies are coming our way. I hope you're proud of that as well.

I find my work meaningful and fun. I get to work with the smartest, most talented, most ingenious teammates. When times have been good, you've been humble. When times have been tough, you've been strong and supportive, and we've made each other laugh. It is a joy to work on this team.

As much as I still tap dance into the office, I'm excited about this transition. Millions of customers depend on us for our services, and more than a million employees depend on us for their livelihoods. Being the CEO of Amazon is a deep responsibility, and it's consuming. When you have a responsibility like that, it's hard to put attention on anything else. As Exec Chair I will stay engaged in important Amazon initiatives but also have the time and energy I need to focus on the Day 1 Fund, the Bezos Earth Fund, Blue Origin, The Washington Post, and my other passions. I've never had more energy, and this isn't about retiring. I'm super passionate about the impact I think these organizations can have.

Amazon couldn't be better positioned for the future. We are firing on all cylinders, just as the world needs us to. We have things in the pipeline that will continue to astonish. We serve individuals and enterprises, and we've pioneered two complete industries and a whole new class of devices. We are leaders in areas as varied as machine learning and logistics, and if an Amazonian's idea requires yet another new institutional skill, we're flexible enough and patient enough to learn it.

Keep inventing, and don't despair when at first the idea looks crazy. Remember to wander. Let curiosity be your compass. It remains Day 1.

Jeff

All these examples of great communication contain genuine care and concern for the people who remain. They have talked about their successors openly and given warm support. The area with the most coverage is about the achievements of the business which include financial stability, minimum wages, returns for stakeholders and improvements to their culture. These are all framed as what *we* (the business) have achieved and not solely claimed by the author of the email. They are also forward looking for the business they are leaving and the success they expect for the people and business. Cynical people may argue that this is a Public Relations exercise and done with subsequent social media coverage in mind. I find this difficult to believe as a disingenuous email will be called out by many current and former employees.

When conducting my research, I was reminded of an email I received from a fantastic HR Director who had secured an internal move. She had a 2-week handover period with her successor and during that time, we all got to meet with him. He was very different. Not just his style, but his personality was completely different to his predecessor. In the 2 weeks we had spent with him, all the senior leadership team had grown worried about the future for our business and our team. One by one, we had sought a final conversation with our former HRD about the future. On her final day, we all received an email. It was incredibly well crafted and I could hear her saying the words. She reminded me and my colleagues that change is a process that we all go through and she did the same as the authors above. She took the time to celebrate our achievements and looked forward to the success we could continue to make as a new team. Her final words were "Time to go." I've never forgotten that email and over the years, I've realised what a great leadership role model I had the privilege to work for. As a leader, our responsibility for communication continues until the last interaction we have in a business and continues afterwards in our gratitude we show to the people we worked with.

The business as a trusted source of information

Have you ever stopped to consider the impact of the communication your business distributes to your employees? As an employer, you have an enormous impact on how employees live their lives as they make decisions on your communications that may continue to impact them for many years to come. This can include decisions on where to live, what careers choices they make, the family they decide to raise and the investments they make through pensions and stocks. These decisions are easy to understand but have you through about the amount of trust that employees have in what you say as a leader?

The Edelman Trust Barometer[27] is a global measure of trust that has been operating for 21 years. The online survey covers 28 countries with over 33,000 respondents and is available at country level. The outcomes of the survey are startling. Overall, people have trust in their business more than in the Government, NGOs and the Media. (In 18 out of 27 countries, business is trusted more than the Government.) The Edelman Trust Barometer goes further than this and identifies that only businesses are both ethical and competent to compared to Governments, NGOs and the Media.

What this gives leaders is a basis of trust. What you communicate to your employees is more likely to be trusted than if it came from your government. Now that's powerful. Because of this, you have an added responsibility to ensure the validity of the messages you send within your business. During a fiscal crisis, pandemic, war or other event that causes wholesale disruption, you have a responsibility to lead your people and provide the support they need to cope with the challenges they face. People will make decisions on your communications that will affect them and their families, for years to come.

Case Study - Communication challenges in a billion-pound business

Iain Fraser, Business Consultant

Together with a number of colleagues from the public and private sector, I worked in a hybrid organisation that had been established to transfer services, that were provided solely by the public sector, into the private sector and therefore open to greater commercial competition and potential savings. This was a multi-billion-pound business which comprised of 3 teams that I'll refer to as A, B and C.

I quickly established that there appeared to be little or no interaction and information sharing between the 3 teams and what limited interactions I observed, appeared to be focused towards limited and specific business outputs. The majority of people in teams A, B and C continued their business focus and output with minimal understanding or knowledge of the other teams. This apparent lack of interaction and communication throughout the business, appeared to me, a newcomer to the business, an issue that warranted further investigation. I led a study into the communication models and the effectiveness of communication, throughout the business with the aim of identifying recommendations to improve the communications and therefore the business outcomes of the organisation.

I started the study with simple observations of the working arrangements which led to semi-structured interviews with key people. Initially, I sensed and experienced a tangible reticence to engage with the study, especially from key individuals from Team B who expressed a personal worry that if they talked to me that they may get into trouble may affect their position and progress in the organisation. This was a false perception, but it was a barrier to gathering important information from sources and viewpoints of colleagues. It appeared that within this organisation a culture of openness and transparency wasn't perceived to be of a high priority.

After several interviews, with a representative cohort from the organisation, it was quite clear that 2 of the 3 teams thought of themselves as separate businesses (Teams B and C), but aligned to the organisation. However, one team viewed themselves as totally independent to the other two despite sharing office space (Team A). Even though they were all part of the same business, there was a feeling that they didn't really belong together. The Teams were geographically located together but there was no shared culture or communication. This may have been a foundational reason why there appeared to be significant barriers to the organisation's internal communication. Even though the Teams, and colleagues from those teams were only metres apart, nobody saw themselves as being part of that one business. Further barriers were created as one team (Team B) wore corporate branded clothes and when entering the office of the other teams, this appearance presented a barrier to meaningful interaction that had to be overcome.

It appeared that there was more sharing of information and general communication within Team C. They had open conversations with each other and regular Townhalls to share information with everyone in their team. A transparent culture of sharing business focus appeared via posters on walls. In Team B, there was no verbal communication. Instead, everything was done by email. There was a perception that once you press click, you've communicated. Regardless of the severity of the message or how important the information was, it was always transmitted by email. In Team B, any team chats were constrained to just a few people, with direct contact to the Director

The impact and the over reliance on emails was clearly articulated by interviewed members of Team B. They felt bombarded with emails, but due to the number of emails, they skimmed read many and sometimes deleted without reading. Even though some of Team B felt isolated from internal communications, the practice of deleting internal communication emails continued as this channel was flooded. Colleagues felt they had no time to read these emails and perceived them as a lower priority than the plethora of work emails. Additionally, many of Team A and B commented that they had given up with trying to understand what was happening within the business and a degree of internal communication apathy was evident. Electronic communication and sharing, between the teams was complex as the 3 teams used separate systems that were unable to be connected with Team C's network

In Team A and B, I noticed that colleagues would rather send an email rather than initiate a conversation, even if the person was in close proximity. It appeared that there was a reluctance to move around the office to communicate and engage with each other and have a productive 2-way conversation.
This prevented people understanding if their message had been received and more importantly understood as they never got to utilise verbal and visual cues that we employ when communicating

The failure in effective communication between the teams and within the teams were a contributing factor in team members feeling disengaged from the organisation's focus and its output, which resulted in key business milestones not being achieved.

Middle and senior leaders commented that they would bypass organisational and business processes, that had been established for governance, to undertake closed door discussions with other senior leaders. This isolated other members of the team from the spreading of key information which would normally flow from the business processes.

Interviewees commented that they would find out about a serious issue when something got brought up at a unplanned briefing event. It appeared that no effort was expended to bring in key elements of the business to deal with an issue, to mitigate it, or seek specialist input from other people to help understand how the issue had arisen. There had been several serious Health & Safety incidents throughout the wider business and it was clear that better communication, understanding and specialist input was required.

Communication was often prevented because colleagues felt an anxiety of over communicating and giving a commercial advantage to Team C. Team A were busy dealing with some of the Health and Safety incidents which meant they shutdown communications even more. This led me to look at which team had a communication strategy which would set out how and when these communications could take place to support all of the teams. I did find that Team C had a communication strategy, Team A didn't have one and Team B had one that was 10 years old.

There was a mixed response to my study. Team A didn't want to know about the outcomes, Team B asked to see a copy of the final report and Team C asked to be kept updated. I believe that the senior leadership was initially supportive of the study, but over time the interest waned as business issues drew the senior leadership teams' focus to other matters.

Overall, the study gave me a great insight into a major business and the issues that can be created within a joint venture. Many of the communication issues could be addressed with some quick wins but there was also a cultural issue that prevented progress.

Iain's case study highlights the issue with bringing different businesses together to form a joint venture. Without an overall plan, the mixture of culture and communication styles clash which then causes tension between the people who are trying to make the new organisation work. The communication in the business failed and they had no plan to bring the teams together so they were aware of one clear vision. In the modern day, their inability to connect their Information Technology systems is clearly an indication that the business will be directly affected and their outcomes will be impeded. In great teams, communication is clear and consistent. This team had not set themselves up for success.

Communication at scale

Since around 2014, there has been a move away from annual appraisals towards a more fluid system of communication with employees. These have often been referred to as check-ins. Regardless of whether you have annual appraisals or check-ins, this is one of the few opportunities where leaders can directly communicate with people across the business.

This is critical to the communication of a leader and how they set the tone for communication across the business. Role modelling of the appraisals and check-ins is key for successful personal communication and should not be underestimated. If you want to explore what disgruntled employees think of their employers, you will quicky establish that 'feedback from my manager' is common theme.

Research carried out by the CEB (Corporate Executive Board that was bought by Gartner) in 2017 found that appraisals cost between £1400-£2400 per year. Whilst some proponents of appraisals will argue that there is always a cost of any system, the CEB also found that 75% of the objectives set were not relevant by the end of the year. Coupled with the wellbeing impact that 40% of respondents thought the appraisal process was too stressful, it's not surprising to see that many leaders have sought to change their process.

Because of the changing expectations of the workforce and the evidence around appraisals, I want to focus on check-ins in this section. The shift from appraisals to more frequent conversations is driven by leaders wanting to get more from their investment of time. My definition of a check-in is '...an open discussion between a manager and employee regarding goals, achievements, career progression, providing/seeking support, celebrating success and development needs.'

The frequency of a check-in is determined by both the manager and employee and not by a set rhythm. Check-ins should be held when they are needed and not a fixed period that may miss key opportunities for great discussions. This sets a check-in aside from an annual appraisal as, given its title, an annual appraisal is only held once per year and is more retrospective.

There will be some occasions where employees have contributed to other projects where the manager is not aware of their direct contribution and may need to include other attendees in the discussion. Check-ins also support cross team working so that an employee's efforts can be fully recognised even where their direct manager is not the lead nor do they have expert knowledge.

Check-ins should be used throughout the year to encourage communicate, feedback and developmental discussions. This may require an immediate check-in if a project has progressed particularly well or there are lessons learned for future projects. Feedback is two-way and should allow for the employee to give feedback to their manager. Feedback helps reinforce the tasks, discover what employees can do better and help track progress.

Expectations can be set by the manager and the employee can understand how they are progressing towards their goals. At a check-in, both employee and manager can check that all expectations are aligned against the business need and realign if necessary. As a tool to support development, check-ins can be used to record the feedback from Conferences, Courses or Networking. This enables 'on time' reviews to take place and plans to be developed for further personal growth.

As check-ins are available through cloud-based software or virtual meetings, they can be conducted for everyone, regardless of location. The discussion may take place through video conferencing and supported in parallel by an online check-in discussion to record the key points. Importantly, there are no limits to the number of check-ins a manager and employee can have during the year.

A manager and employee can use the check-in to have honest and rich discussions about their work. The focus for each may be slightly different depending on who has scheduled the check-in but here are some questions for both the manager and employee to consider. These may act as a catalyst for a conversation and avoid an awkward silence.

Figure 4.2 – Check-in questions

	Manager	**Employee**
Induction	What have you enjoyed in your first 30/60/90 days?	I'd like to discuss more about the key stakeholders in the business and how I can interact with them.
	Do you have what you need to do your job?	Do we have a mentor scheme I can access?
	How are you settling into the team?	Who are your role models in the business and why?
	What communication would you prefer from me, so you are able to do your job?	Where are the pitfalls I should avoid?
Individual	How can I provide better support for you?	How am I perceived throughout the business?
	Are there any blockers or obstacles I can remove for you?	I've been looking at a vacancy within/outside of the company....
	How can I work differently to enable you to work better?	I have reflected on our last check-in....
	What should I stop doing and what should I start doing?	What do I need to improve on?
Talent	How do you see your career progressing?	I'd like to discuss a development opportunity that I believe would assist me within my role.....
	I have reviewed your benefits and rewards.......	What fast-track schemes are in place that I could benefit from?
	What areas of your daily work do you wish to strengthen?	Would you support my application for access to the future leaders' programme?
	What development have you done recently to support your career goals?	What is holding me back from progressing in my career?
Performance	How are you progressing with your projects?	This job isn't working out how I expected. Can we discuss my options?
	How are your people performing?	I've encountered some problems on a recent project.....
	I'd like to discuss your performance since we last met.....	I'd like to brief my staff about.....

	I have received some feedback about your involvement in a project.....	I've completed a project and I have capacity to progress to the next project. What is next?
Opportunity	What development needs have you identified for yourself?	Are there any other opportunities to get involved in other projects as I'd like to progress within the company....
	There is a vacancy I think you would be ideally suited for......	I'm not being stretched in this job. Can I take on other responsibilities or is there another jo for me?
	I've had a request for a contribution to a video/article which will be published in the national press. Would you like to take part?	I've been asked to support my professional body, but it may need some support during the working day. Can we discuss?
	There is a secondment available within another department that would help with your development. Would you like to discuss?	I've been offered a job at a rival business. Can we discuss my options here or a way I can leave in a positive way?

There is an amazing quote by Dave Ulrich from his book 'Victory Through Organisations'[28], he said that 'feedback is a leader's primary responsibility, not a side responsibility'. Dave's comment took check-ins and leadership communication to the next level for me as a leader. Your primary role is to give people the feedback. That changed my behaviour and my approach to leadership.

Summary

Communication is a key part of being a leader. Like many other leadership competencies, you can only develop this by practice, gaining feedback and refining your approach next time. But don't confuse this with simply being the 'good news' leader. There will be occasions when you need to deliver tough messages that not everyone will like. These occasions demand a clarity of message, delivered in a professional manner and the openness to discuss what this means for people.

Reflective activities

- Think back to some great pieces of communication in your business. What made it special? What can you learn from this?
- When you communicate do you consider the impact it might have and how it might be interpreted? Have you asked anyone about how your last communication was received?
- Is providing feedback one of your strengths or weaknesses? How could you improve on this?

Suggested reading

- Nadella S. (2018). *Hit Refresh*. Williams Collins. UK: London.
- Hoffman Y. (2020). *Beyond Engagement*. Authors Place Press. USA: Colorado.

Part 2

Making an impact

Chapter 5

Culture

"There's no magic formula for great company culture. The key is just to treat your staff how you would like to be treated."
Richard Branson (Founder, Virgin Group)

Introduction

The culture of an organisation is not measured in how many ping-pong tables a business owns. It is not about free sweets or breakfast. (The free food is there to get you in early so you can do more work without extra pay; food is cheaper than an overtime payment!) Culture is a subject that has as many viewpoints as there are authors. My own view is that culture is difficult to measure, it is possible to shape, it cannot be owned by one person and it absolutely has a direct effect on the outcomes of a business and the people it employs.

Glassdoor provides some insight into the effect of a culture on a business and its current/former employees. Salesforce is currently rated as the top employer on Glassdoor with a rating of 4.4/5 and with a 97% approval of the CEO, Marc Benioff. Of their 10,000 reviews, 435 mention their 'great culture'. The reviewers talk about their great culture in conjunction with a variety of other benefits including collaborative atmosphere, growth opportunities, career guidance, welfare and work-life balance. After reviewing Glassdoor's top 10 best places to work[29], culture features heavily in the reviews for each company.

Business culture is an area of real interest for me as I have seen the effects a poor culture has on a team and a business. One of the discussions I often get into is the level of control leaders have over the culture within their business. To explore this further, I ran a survey with over 100 global leaders (across EMEA, APAC and the US) and asked, "Do you actively manage your organisation's culture?". Here are the results:

Yes	52%
No	7%
Somewhat	23%
It's not possible	18%

This tells me that 75% of leaders are trying to manage their culture – as they answered, 'yes' or 'somewhat'. If you're part of the 25% who feel it is not possible or you just don't try to manage it, you're not going to feature in the next Glassdoor list of top 10 businesses. In this chapter, I want to help the 75% do what they do better and challenge the 25% of leaders to really look at why they need to amend their approach.

In this chapter I will look at several splendid examples of transparency within businesses as this is an indicator of culture. My focus is on transparency as it is a key part of an open culture that acts as a foundation for other behaviours and actions that then build a great culture. This chapter will consider why and how a leader can create a culture where people feel able to challenge decisions and take actions without the need for layers of hierarchy.

Why should a leader create a great culture?

Let's start with some statistics for this section. You can easily find your own research papers and do your own analysis on culture but here are some compelling findings from well-known institutions:

- 88% of employees believe a distinct workplace culture is important to business success.[30]

- Companies with strong cultures saw a 4x increase in revenue growth.[31]

- 58% of people say they trust strangers more than their own boss.[32]

- When companies have a poor culture, 48% employees start looking for a job.[33]

- 78% of executives said culture is among the top five things that add value to their company.[34]

Additionally, it has been found that happy workers are 13% more productive[35] and having a culture that supports happy workers makes it easier to recruit new people. If you did not already know, your competitors are already using their culture to attract the same talent. They are working hard to make sure their people talk about the culture within the business and how they feel about working in that culture. Your competitors will use any advantage they have to get the best people. Here are extracts from some adverts in different industries showing this in action:

- *Test Manager - As well as doing great work, we are creating a place that is great to do work in. We offer tip-top kit, brilliant training opportunities and support from expert colleagues. On top of that, you will find flexible working, an inclusive culture and a place where your opinion is valued.*

- *Product Designer - We are committed to building an inclusive culture and to creating an environment where people can balance successful careers with their commitments and interests outside of work.*

- *Head of HR - Culture is key for this business, they work hard but have fun whilst doing it and importantly they class results as more important than time worked.*

- *Consultant - Providing an unparalleled company culture, we will help you to be the best that you can be. From access to the latest technology, training and accreditation to keep you at the top of your game, through to flexible working to fit your lifestyle and health and well-being initiatives to keep you feeling great.*

- *Architect - You'll learn, grow and advance in an innovative culture that thrives on shared success, diverse ways of thinking and enables boundaryless opportunities that can drive your career in new and exciting ways.*

- *Director - We take pride in our inspirational organizational culture and offer a fun and engaging environment to help our employees bring their best selves to work every single day. Our work family is important to us and we regularly take time to connect and have fun together as a team.*

- *Brand Ambassador - Our company culture - we won best company to work for in 2019 and our CEO, Greg has recorded a podcast about our culture and how we empower our people.*

- *Account Specialist - Our culture is innovative and collaborative - where bold ideas turn into action. We grow strong talent through stretch opportunities only restricted by your interests.*

Now review your job adverts and see if there is a difference. If you're not mentioning your culture you are not giving a key piece of business information to your candidates about the jobs they are considering. In such a tight market to attract candidates, you should seek to use every advantage you have including your business culture. Indeed[36] (one of the world's leading job sites) provides some great advice about using your company culture to 'hook' candidates. This advice from Indeed is summarised into the following key areas to look at when creating a job advert:

- Use language that caters to the candidate.
- Avoid using clichés and buzzwords.
- Highlight things that make your employees happy.
- Mention flexible hours and remote/hybrid work.
- Describe office design or location benefits.

- Promote career development.
- Show you understand the importance of their work.
- Highlight a collaborative office culture.

Now review the examples I have provided above and see how many of these pieces of advice have been used in the adverts. The answer is that none of the job adverts contain all the points but they have some of them. Finding a balance between over-selling the culture which would look suspicious to under-selling the culture which would be a missed opportunity is one of the enduring issues for most recruitment teams. If this is going to be your first attempt to describe your culture in a job advert, take some time to review other job adverts and write several versions of what you want to describe. Then, ask some of your recent hires if they thought your description matches the business. You may also find out more about the realities of your culture.

Once you have successfully recruited great people who buy-in to the culture you have described, you need to keep them. It will be these people that make your business successful and deliver the outcomes you need to grow and thrive as a business. This includes creating an environment that supports retention of your people which is a competitive advantage for your business. Get your culture right, and your people will also be the reason that others want to join you or it will be the reason your competitors want to be you. Research has proven the link between culture and higher productivity and Gallup[37] have a proven range of performance metrics to show this link:

- 50-point increase in employee engagement over a three-year period.
- 25% growth in workforce over a three-year period.
- 85% net profit increase over a five-year period.
- 138% improvement in patronage over a five-year period.

Once you have started the journey towards a great culture, your next challenge is to ensure it is not diluted or held-back by the wrong people. Professor Robert Sutton[38] wrote 'The No Asshole Rule' in 2010 to explain his beliefs about assholes in the workplace. It's self-explanatory and many businesses strive to achieve this by actively rooting out the assholes in their business. There are other terms for this – often seen as more acceptable – which include brilliant jerks and high-on-performance-bad-on-attitude. Arianna Huffington[39], CEO of Thrive, said about brilliant jerks "The truth is they end up affecting the whole culture. Even if they may individually create results, they end up having a negative impact on the business."

You cannot lead brilliant jerks in the long-term and the good intentions of turning them around to be positive influences is often a wasted effort. As a leader, you should decide what your tolerance level is and then ensure you have a robust process to get rid of these assholes so your work on developing a great culture is not undone.

> **Leadership Tip**
>
> *"Our number one priority is company culture. Our whole belief is that if you get the culture right, most of the other stuff like delivering great customer service or building a long-term enduring brand will just happen naturally on its own."*
> *Tony Hsieh (Former CEO, Zappos)*

Business cultures

You may have read articles and stories about businesses explaining their culture but the standout effort for me remains the 2009 PowerPoint presentation by Netflix[40]. Since they were released, I've read these slides on many occasions, sent them to other leaders and referenced them in articles/presentations. They remain a great example of a business trying to record their culture on paper and making it a part of people's induction. For the detractors who have failed to discuss their culture with new starters because they believe it is impossible to write down a culture, here's an example of why you should try. If you have not looked at these slides, take the time to find them on the internet and make your own assessment. In the meantime, here's my assessment of the Netflix culture slides.

The first area that struck me was the link to values. They are so under-used and often created at great expense. Right from the outset, Netflix are saying that their values matter and here's why they are the centre point of our culture. So often, I seen values as an afterthought or created just to tick a box on some accreditation process. The norm is for people not to know the business values or that they even exist.

Netflix's 'seven aspects of our culture' is summed up in one slide:

- Values are what we value.
- High Performance.
- Freedom and responsibility.
- Context, not control.
- Highly aligned, loosely coupled.
- Pay top of market.
- Promotions and development.

What then follows is a detailed explanation about the tests they apply as a manager to their staff including 'The Keeper Test'. They are encouraged to ask themselves "Which of my people, if they told me they were leaving in two months for a similar job at a peer company, would I fight hard to keep at Netflix?". Netflix then also look at getting rid of people for average performance to open a slot for another star. For them, average people "should get a generous severance now" as they advise that a focus on performance supports 2x better performance from people in procedural roles and 10x better performance from people in creative roles.

As part of their freedom and responsibility aspect of culture, Netflix do not track or record vacations. Neither do they have a dress code. They have a quote in their slides from Patty McCord, former Chief Talent Office at Netflix, (2004) which advises "There is also no clothing policy at Netflix, but no one has come to work naked lately." The slides also set out a clear understanding of personal responsibility – see their 5-word expenses policy! This is really set out in personal development which puts the responsibility entirely on the individual. It is a great foundation for any business as Netflix considers that formal courses rarely reap the learning experience that is intended. Netflix advise that "Individuals should manage their own career path, and not rely on a corporation for planning their careers." This self-interest around personal development stands out for me as it is a belief I have held for many years. After starting my career and naively believing that I would be looked after and planned for centrally, I soon learned that it was me who was responsible for my learning pathway and direction of my career.

Netflix also embrace the informal learning approach as they note that "high performance people are generally self-improving through experience, observation, introspection, reading and discussion. As long as they have stunning colleagues and big challenges." This blunt cultural approach, including their pay strategy, may drive some people away or shorten their time at Netflix but it is rare to see such openness about their approach to such topics. I would like to see a session conducted with all school, college and university leavers to explain to them that they are the only ones who are responsible for their career development and that leaving your personal development to the whim of a business is a guarantee to go nowhere.

There are other examples of good culture that you may be aware of. Whilst writing this book, I saw a post on LinkedIn which read:

"One of the organisations I work with has just announced a meeting light fortnight, with strong encouragement to cancel all non-essential meetings during this time to give people a break from spending so much time online. Stuff like this can send a strong message. More please!"

This is leadership at work, seeing an issue and then addressing it. Examples like this are key to building a great culture. Here are a few other stand-out elements from different cultures.

- Zappos (Online retailer) offer some employees $2000 to quit after only a few weeks if they don't like the job. There's no animosity. Just a straightforward business deal that sees the employee free up their space so they can fill it with a better candidate and it hasn't taken months of poor performance, management distraction and team disruption to achieve the same effect.

- Rapha (Cycling clothing) has a range of cultural benefits listed in their adverts. This includes "...a flexible riding benefit to allow you to go out riding on a Wednesday morning with colleagues or learn to cycle through our Getting Started Scheme." and "No meeting Fridays - giving you time back for things like personal development."

- Sony[41] (Music) describe how their 'What if' committee lead many activities within the businesses as "Our staff committee What if? takes the lead on a range of diversity, environmental workplace and social initiatives. What if? has helped Sony minimise the use of plastic, introduced Premium Days for staff personal development, hosted talks with top talent and promotes wellbeing through regular activities such as yoga classes, mindfulness and Gospeloke." They also have a clear focus on development which states "Sony Music helps employees progress their career at every stage. We take professional and personal development seriously and offer a range of award-winning programmes to help everyone thrive."

- Lenovo[42] (Information Technology) have a model which is present throughout their business. "Our culture defines us ... it's our DNA. We call it the Lenovo Way and it's the values we share and the business practices we deploy. It's how we address our day-to-day commitments. The Lenovo Way is embodied in the statement: We do what we say and we own what we do. That culture also drives how we work every day, utilizing what we call the 5 P's:

    - We PLAN before we pledge.
    - We PERFORM as we promise.
    - We PRIORITIZE the company first.
    - We PRACTICE improving every day.
    - We PIONEER new ideas."

- REI[43] (Retailer) offers sabbaticals to help their team celebrate their tenure with the company. On a 15-year service anniversary, employees will earn a consecutive four-week, company-paid sabbatical. This repeats every five years. Also, the REI Yay Day program allows employees, twice a year, to partake in their favourite outdoor pursuit, take on a new activity or participate in a stewardship project.

- Adobe[44] (Software) match donations of time and treasure to eligible non-profits and schools. They provide employees with funds and opportunities to act in their local community, and they also tie pro bono projects and non-profit board service to people's professional development plans. This helps build a culture of local assistance and encourages their employees to give service to non-profits outside of work.

- Pixar[45] (Animation Studio) use unfinished work as a vehicle to build collaboration and drive a creative culture. By sharing the unfinished work, it gives other people the chance to display talent and shows a willingness to be vulnerable. When combined, this helps build an open culture but also helps to progress projects that could otherwise remain in a state of paralysis.

An area I wish to draw your attention to is the frequency of people tying their culture to their values. The link between setting out values and then living through the culture, directly affects how the culture is then perceived internally and externally.

The Glassdoor[46] top 14 businesses with the best cultures and values in the UK are a variety of businesses across all sectors but the ones that standout are Cloudreach, Lookers, Booking.com, O2 and Sky Betting and Gaming. Feel free to disagree with me on this selection, as we all have different expectations of a great culture and the measures we use to determine if a business has a good culture.

I hope you can see what others have done to drive their business and that they have done what is right for them. I'm sure that as you have read some of these examples that many of these cultural tools would not work in your business. That is OK! You cannot transpose one culture onto another and expect it to work – there are many examples of failed mergers and acquisitions that stand testament to this. You should be able to assimilate these examples and assess what would work in your business. It may not be the same. It could be the same theme but adjusted for your environment. To review this area more specifically, you need to research what your competition are doing to drive their culture but also be aware of national boundaries. Multi-national companies have greater considerations where their approach needs some element of localisation to prevent an extended difference given the local economy and that of the 'home' territory.

How many levels of hierarchy exist in your business?

Hierarchies are an important symbol of a business culture. Consider how many levels of hierarchy exist in your business and the challenges this can cause. How many levels of hierarchy do you think the following businesses have? (The answers are at the end of the chapter.)

Figure 5.1 – Numbers of hierarchy

Business	Levels of hierarchy
Civil Service	
British Army	
Police	
Tesco	
Google	
Facebook	
HSBC	
Football Association (Leagues)	
Add your business here!	

Throughout history, civilisations have developed based on hierarchies of people. This has often been based on power – physical power – as leaders battled for the leadership of their village/tribe. We also see hierarchies amongst animals and the same physical battles for supremacy. Some leaders have been appointed because of their ability to lead people to war, others for their visionary abilities and some for the resources they bring to the group. Hierarchies have been cemented by weddings between two powerful families both within local areas and between countries to help forge an alliance and secure power for another generation.

Politics is a clear example of people joining groups to create hierarchies which keep out rival hierarchies. They are designed to be self-serving and repel any attack. They can also be the cause of in-decision, lack of adaptability and poor communication as insecure leaders appoint extra levels of management to insulate themselves from people who may challenge their authority.

It is because of these issues that many businesses have chosen to flatten their structures or completely throw away the notion of a hierarchy. How does that make you feel when you think about stripping out the layers of hierarchy in your business? Enthused or confused? In 2018[47], both Sainsbury's and Tesco completed delayering across their stores in the UK. Sainsbury decided to remove team leader and store supervisor jobs to deliver savings of around £500M over the following 3 years.

Around the same time Tesco[48] also announced their intention to cut 1700 management positions as part of a £1.5Bn package of savings over the following 3 years. For anyone setting out on this journey to delayer their business, the guiding principle is to delayer from the top, not the bottom.

It is often the upper and middle management layers that have grown fat, often through 'honour' promotions, and are the areas most in need of change. Delayering the lower levels of the business is an easy route to failure as this is where most of the competitive advantage is delivered.

Large businesses, such as retailers, grow to a size where delayering is the right option to streamline new processes or embrace the use of new technology. The numbers of people involved are always large and the extent of the change is nationwide given their amount of sites. Many businesses have set out to retain a flat structure which reduces the costs, helps to remain agile but most of all, makes communication much quicker. For start-ups, the key ingredient is growth is to get feedback from within the business, partners or customers and then act upon it. As businesses grow and develop complex hierarchies, the speed of communications slows and bureaucracy tends to define how quickly decision can be taken. CEOs will often run catch-up sessions (focus groups, coffee hours etc) with a handful of people so they can circumvent the traditional filters to gain first-hand feedback from around their business. These sessions are a quick way of getting a temperature check but getting fully rounded feedback takes more time.

As I have already discussed, some of the largest retailers in the UK have been delayering their business from a cost-saving perspective. Here are some examples of businesses where the flat structure is at the heart of their business:

- Square Space - This successful start-up is regularly voted as one of the best places to work in New York City. Its company culture is one that is "flat, open and creative." A flat organization is one where there are no (or very few) levels of management in between staff and executives. This approach is more common among start-ups and can be tricky to maintain as a company grows larger, requiring groups to form.

- Adobe - Adobe is a company that goes out of its way to give employees challenging projects and then provide the trust and support to help them meet those challenges successfully. While it offers benefits and perks like any modern creative company, Adobe's is a culture that avoids micromanaging in favour of trusting employees to do their best.

- Nike[49] – Although Nike operates a flat structure in conjunction with matrix management to help deliver new products, the overall focus is on faster decision making which allows for innovative ideas to be quickly assessed. This also helps smaller teams in different regions to react quicker to local trends and preferences.

- Gumroad[50] – This is a small start-up in Silicon Valley which started with 20 people reporting directly to their CEO and Founder Sahil Lavingia. They provide a platform for creators to sell their apps, images, memberships and many other items to a wide customer base. With their flat structure, they react quickly to the needs of their 93,000 creators and have helped to sell over $493M of product through their site.

A flatter organisation can also help to shape your company culture to a more open and challenging culture where people are confident to challenge assumptions and decisions. Gumroad is a notable example where they use communication tools to have 1-2-1 discussions between colleagues but they are all open and accessible by everyone in the business to encourage sharing and prevent knowledge being locked up in emails. These further drives positive challenge and contribution from others who would have been excluded from the discussion in other businesses.

A lack of transparency

The internet has given businesses and every person the opportunity to demonstrate transparency. Despite the omni-present internet, some still seek to blur and obscure their activities leading to scandal and prosecutions. The Ranking Digital Rights Corporate Accountability Index (2018)[51] evaluates 22 of the world's most powerful internet, mobile, and telecommunications companies on their disclosed commitments and policies affecting freedom of expression and privacy.
This includes businesses such as Microsoft, Facebook, Google, Orange, Vodaphone and Samsung. According to the report, "Companies are not transparent enough about the design, management, and governance of digital platforms and services that affect human rights."

In 2018, a former employee of Cambridge Analytica, disclosed they had harvested the data of 87 million Facebook accounts and then used the information to provide analytical assistance to the 2016 campaign of Donald Trump. The lack of transparency about how people's data is being used by the big tech companies was a wake-up call for many people. Facebook were fined $5 billion dollars in the US and £500,000 in the UK for the privacy violations whilst Cambridge Analytica filed for bankruptcy in 2018.

Boeing's issues with the 737 Max[52], which had suffered two fatal crashes with the deaths of 346 people, raised issues around corporate culture and lack of transparency. The culture was lacking on several counts including an unhealthy focus on profits, an arrogance towards the regulators and a less than acceptable approach to safety concerns. Following several government investigations, the entire fleet was grounded but the CEO, Dennis Muilenburg, continued to be optimistic about the future of the 737 Max which led to a PR disaster.

There was a lack of transparency over the issues Boeing were facing. The issues were in part due to a poor design and the failing culture that had surrounded the debacle. After Muilenburg resigned in December 2019, Boeing endured two years of intense work to re-establish itself as a trustworthy manufacturer for both the airline industry and their passengers. The 737 Max scandal cost Boeing around $20 billion in fines and compensation and a further $60 billion in cancelled orders.

How do I create transparency?

There are some incredible examples where businesses have stepped out of the darkness of secrecy to explain to their employees, customers and stakeholders how they reward their people. It's the most delicate subject at work and often the subject of many rules or policies about how/when salaries can be discussed. Dan Price at Gravity Payments is one example and in Chapter 3, I talked about his drive to set $70k as their minimum wage. Throughout this journey, he has been vocal about the change he has made, the cut in salary he took to achieve this and then persisted with his challenge to other businesses.

Dan's passion for paying people is incredible. But there is an even greater example. In 2015 I was exploring how I could use social media in a more professional and focused way to help build my profile to help drive sales. I had spent many hours looking at different apps and researched how to get the most out of the platforms I felt comfortable with.
Eventually, I found Buffer. I started to use Buffer for scheduling my LinkedIn posts and Tweets (I've just released a secret that some people were not aware of) so I could be 'present' across different time zones with my content. I had been using Buffer for over a year when I found in the footer notes on their website a link to 'Salaries'.

Incredibly, they publish the formula they use to calculate a salary and publish the salaries of all their people. They simply take a benchmark for a role (e.g. Customer advocate III at $106,912) multiply it by a cost-of-living factor (e.g. intermediate band of 90%) which then gives a salary. In this example, the Customer Advocate III with an intermediate location band would have a salary of $96,220.

Whilst the Buffer example is an outlier in terms of its public pay policy, in the UK the Localism Act 2011[53], requires a 'relevant authority' to publish a Pay Policy Statement which sets out the pay for senior members of the department. The Act states that:

> A relevant authority must prepare a pay policy statement for the financial year 2012-2013 and each subsequent financial year.
>
> > (2)A pay policy statement for a financial year must set out the authority's policies for the financial year relating

to—

(a)the remuneration of its chief officers,

(b)the remuneration of its lowest-paid employees, and

(c)the relationship between—

(i)the remuneration of its chief officers, and

(ii)the remuneration of its employees who are not chief officers.

This gives an insight into the pay of senior leaders across the country and is freely available on the websites of Councils etc. If you're not aware this is available, here's 10 salaries of Council CEOs around the country:

Figure 5.2 – CEO pay in Councils

	Salary
Nottinghamshire County Council	£185,386
Derbyshire County Council	£150,554 - £164,728
East Sussex County Council	£200,000 - £204,999
Cornwall County Council	£185,384
Northumberland County Council	£195,000 - £199,999
Kent County Council	£207,884
Surrey County Council	£214,184 - £237,337
Lancashire County Council	£216,826

There are few examples of private business having such a transparent salary system but it is easier to find the Public Sector salaries. Some businesses actively seek to obscure their salaries or prevent employees from discussing their reward package. Publishing salaries is the ultimate in an open culture but it still does not define an open culture. There are many more behaviours and actions that are needed for a business to have a great culture.

When you have been reading this section on published salaries, how have you felt? Did you reel at the thought or your colleagues seeing your salary? I've discussed this with many businesses and groups of people just to see their reactions. The uneasy shuffling of feet, wincing and dismissal of the idea to an eagerness to hear more and what this would mean for them and their business. The introduction of Buffer's approach may help many people achieve pay parity as businesses cannot hide the inequality that would otherwise happen. This approach has been heralded by some as a solution to the gender pay gap.

If you're wondering what happens when a business is not transparent over their salaries and people start to question the executive rewards, Blizzard Entertainment, a division of Activision Blizzard Inc., is a case study worth reviewing. In August 2020[54], reports surfaced of a revolt by the Blizzard employees who were concerned that pay disparity was increasing for the more junior employees.

A shared spreadsheet was soon circulated and employees anonymously added their salary and pay rise details so they could create their own way of transparent salaries. This news was covered extensively by many outlets and 9 months after the reports further revelations revealed a poor work culture where pay imbalances were a smaller issue compared with claims of sexual discrimination and sexual harassment[55]. In 2021[56], the unrest amongst the employees led to a walk out amid renewed complaints of sexual harassment and sexism. J Allen Brack, President of Activision Blizzard, stepped down after accusations that he had not done enough to tackle the poor culture.

Activision Blizzard[57] have now appointed Jen O'Neal and Mike Ybarra to jointly lead the company. The company announced that "Both leaders are deeply committed to all of our employees; to the work ahead to ensure Blizzard is the safest, most welcoming workplace possible for women, and people of any gender, ethnicity, sexual orientation, or background; to upholding and reinforcing our values; and to rebuilding your trust. With their many years of industry experience and deep commitment to integrity and inclusivity, Jen and Mike will lead Blizzard with care, compassion, and a dedication to excellence." I noted that in this statement, the mention of values and trust are the elements that they have identified as key areas to restore and build upon.

Transparency is created by some simple actions that have disproportionate effects. If you're looking to create a more transparent business, consider the following:

- Do we publish our financial statements internally for everyone to consume and see the impact of their work?

- Do we run a staff survey? If so, do we openly publish the results, even when they are uncomfortable, so people can see the feedback and where we need to improve?

- Do we encourage honest feedback at all levels throughout the business?

- Are we honest with our people even if there is bad news?

- Do we communicate clearly and regularly about the future of the business, challenges, successes and failures?

As with all elements of culture, what works for Buffer may not work for you for a variety of reasons. You may be reading this in a business which would not survive the scrutiny of your competitors having free access to your salaries or you may be in a location where such openness would contravene state or federal laws. As a leader, you need to start with a mindset of transparency. Challenge what is not transparent and continually ask why? In a LinkedIn article[58] I explained that 'why?' is the most powerful question a leader can ask and this is exactly the right time to deploy this tactic! The culture you have is the culture you are prepared to accept and you must be the catalyst to change this. If you have the chance to discuss the levels of transparency within your business, with employees, customers, suppliers or partners, then do so. If the opportunity is not readily available, create the opportunity so you can gauge how transparent your business is when viewed through the eyes of your stakeholders. Make the time to challenge your fellow leaders and drive better practices between your leadership team. Do not let people block your road to increasing transparency and act decisively when you identify a blocker. Transparency is such a key ingredient to your culture that you cannot afford to be passive.

What culture is right for my organisation?

You cannot simply lift a culture and apply it to a different business. This should be the first line of any book that claims to have solution for all your cultural issues. Taking the ping pong tables from one business, the 'take as much holiday as you want' from another, the pay transparency of Buffer and mimicking the electric personality of an incredible CEO will not make your business have a great culture. Also, you cannot just lift and shift the whole culture of a business and expect that it will work. For football fans, this is an easy one to understand. How many times have clubs tried to buy a new defence by simply taking 2 or 3 players from a club and hoping this would solve their issues? It does not work because they players need to fit in with those around them and the style of play is vastly different to what helped make them successful at their previous club.

There are many factors at play that affect a culture including: industry, history and geography. I'm going to add a further six factors which are explained in detail by Johnson et al[59] in their Cultural Web. These are: stories, symbols, power structures, organisational structures, control systems and routines & rituals. (If you want to read more about cultures then I recommend you explore the Cultural Web.) The relevance of some of these factors may not be immediately clear so here's my summary on why these should matter to you:

- **Industry** – Some of the older industries have long established cultures stretching back to when they were formed. I've worked in many businesses and provided consultancy for businesses where their industry has not changed since their early days. They may be seen as old fashioned but that is their way and they are still successful. Be sure to understand the industry you work in and the ways of working that may not have changed.

- **History** – There are many new businesses that have been created in the last 10 years. Think about some of the tech companies, space flights, ride shares, parcel deliveries and e-scooters. Many of these businesses have started from just a garage with a few friends that have worked to turn an idea into a global business. As the formed, they had the opportunity to consider their values and culture. Other businesses, car manufacturers, energy companies and banks have been established for many years and have been subject to countless mergers and acquisitions that brought other business together to form what we see today. The history of the business is the foundation for what you have now and what you will build in the future. Reach out to people who have vast corporate knowledge and this may include people who have already retired.

- **Geography** – Different national cultures and behavioural norms affect a business culture. Working in a global business is a matter of understanding the culture of the business and the local business culture. I spoke with a contractor who was asked to complete some building work in a Japanese manufacturing plant in the UK. He visited the site to provide an estimate but once their site manager had explained how they expected them to work, behave and store their tools, he rejected the job and left. The cultural norms the Japanese manufacturer was trying to impose on their contractors was an imbalance with the local practices. (I'm not sure how long they took to find a contractor to do the work to their procedures but their requirements would have led to a drawn out project.)

- **Stories** – The stories are the most powerful part of a culture and often immortalize heroic acts by employees. Larry Page and Sergey Brin's story of building Google in a garage and then Yahoo rejecting the chance to buy their start-up for $1m in 1998 is a great example. Each business will have its own stories of deals won/lost, when people went above and beyond to deliver great customer service or when a business looked after the family of an employee after a fatal accident. Good businesses with strong cultures harness these stories, remind people of the stories and use them to underscore the culture they strive to build.

- **Symbols** – This can be both a negative and positive effect on culture. We often see reserved parking spaces, executive dining rooms or even executive lifts as affecting cultures negatively. But some symbols that build culture are easy to achieve and have huge meaning. Boots gives it is long serving employees golden badges to celebrate their years of service, Southwest airlines encourage their airline stewards to add their own personality to their pre-flight announcements and the welcome packages that businesses now give to new starters which are much talked about and shared on social media.

- **Power structures** – Power often exists in the hands of a few people. Access to the power structures and the way they can be communicated with often sets the tone for the culture. Leaders need to understand who holds the real power, how they can influence the holders of power and the politics behind gaining power. This may be an unsavoury side of culture for many people but unless you learn how to harness the power structures within your business, it will be difficult to succeed.

- **Organisational structures** – The organisation chart that is shown in PowerPoints or held on the HR system is more of a representation of who authorises absences within the business rather than the power structures within the business. The real structures and networks are the ones that are not written down and that grow in the shadows. Often linked with power structures, the organisation structures, both informal and formal, are crucial factors to understand. I was discussing the differences between industries with a business founder and she discussed the challenges she had faced in the hospitality industry. She had discovered, to her cost, that when one staff member left for another job at a newly opened hotel, they were accompanied by 11 other employees who were all related to the first leaver. Until that day, she had no idea they were all related.

- **Control systems** – Employees will have first-hand experience the reward system and the distribution of bonuses. These are examples of control systems. Whilst many people will understand such control systems, it will be fewer people, often the leadership team, that understand and experience day-to-day controls such as procurement systems, financial authority and quality systems. Good leaders must immerse themselves in the running of the business to be more effective than their peers. Without knowledge of these control systems and the gatekeepers that need to be influenced, leaders will struggle to achieve the outcomes they desire. This element of the cultural web is often classed as 'red tape' or 'bureaucracy' and many judgements will be made about the culture on this element alone.

- **Routines & rituals** – This is what happens daily and what behaviour is expected. It may be a specific way of working or how communications are handled that is unique to that business even though they operate in a standardised industry. Some businesses have a specific routine around how rosters are produced and how the prime shifts are spread around the workforce to ensure parity of treatment. Many businesses have their own rituals for retirees and how they celebrate their service to the business. The routines and rituals are practices that people use as a reference point and link very closely to the stories. New starters are often told about the routines and rituals long before their first day or they have read about them in online reviews.

I have provided the cultural factors for you to consider but this is not formulaic. If you are working in a start-up, you can shape how your business grows and consider these factors. In an established business, your challenge will be more about shaping than setting out these factors. As expected, the leadership team will naturally create many aspects of these cultural factors and their behaviour will define how other people act within the business. Leadership role modelling will determine how your culture grows and shifts as successive leaders apply their own approach to the business. In many ways, creating the right culture is like making friends. If you don't try, you will not be successful in growing in the way you hoped for. If you try too hard, you will be seen as fake and people will distance themselves from you.

I've always believed that a few key factors of culture have a disproportionate effect on the overall culture - this could be positive or negative.

Never lose the history of the business even if your business is merged with another. People want to remember their place in the growth of the business and have many stories attached to their contribution to where the business is today. Because of this, the stories created in the business are incredibly powerful and should be harnessed. Take the time to write down the stories and talk about them in the induction for new people. Let them hear about the achievements of their predecessors, by name if possible, and let them start to tell stories about the current people. Finally, power structures are critical to making a business work. They can help to deliver change quickly, support a customer requirement and act as a marketing asset both internally and externally. They can also be destructive, divisive and obstructive. There are times when some power structures need to be disbanded for the good of the rest of the culture and so new power structures can flourish. Just as you would publicise some of your stories to build a culture, never be afraid to challenge a power structure to break up a negative part of the culture that has arisen.

Summary

Finally, culture is a tool for recruiting and retaining employees, and HR managers know that the right culture can foster productivity, engagement, and innovation. Good leaders aspire to developing their leadership style that shapes the culture of the organization and therefore, leads to the success of the business. Leading a good culture is based on authentic leadership which is driven through role modelling and transparency. Leaders can grow and shape their culture without using traditional leadership command and control approaches. They can choose to lead by using components of the leadership paradigm that include flatter structures, transparent processes and value shaped by a variety of stakeholders and not just a few executives. Employees are more likely to support an organization if they feel they have a role to play and values that encourage efforts in their roles and responsibilities. Existing leadership cultures can act as a bottleneck for candidates as people tend to appoint in their shadow. This can perpetuate the same leadership culture that the business is seeking to change.

Leaders shape the culture through conscious and unconscious actions which can result in unintended consequences. The critical factor to shaping a culture is role modelling by a leader. Whatever is agreed as a way forward, or set out in the values of the business, need to then be lived by the leaders. Role modelling is needed at all levels in the business and not just at the CEO level. Leaders throughout the business who may not regard themselves as leaders could be displaying the values more often than people with leadership titles. These people need to be cherished and encourage to progress.

Culture is a living aspect of a business. It should be appreciated, grown, shaped and monitored for any issues. As a leader, you cannot delegate the role modelling of the culture and it is this leading by example that will deliver changes quickly or undermine your business if ignored.

Reflective activities

- Visit your competitor's websites and read their job adverts. How many of them mention their culture in the job adverts?

- Apply the Netflix Keep Test to your team. "Which of my people, if they told me they were leaving in two months for a similar job at a peer company, would I fight hard to keep at Netflix?".

- What do you define as a great culture and what measures do you use to determine this? What businesses do you believe have great cultures?

- How could your business operate with fewer levels of hierarchy? What would be the impact on your customers?

- Do you need all your layers of hierarchy and how would you benefit from removing just one layer?

Levels of Hierarchy

Business	Levels of hierarchy
Civil Service	11
British Army	18
Police	9
Tesco	7
Google	11
Facebook	9
HSBC	9
Football Association (Leagues)	7
Add your business here!	

Suggested reading

- Johnson et al. *Exploring Strategy*. (2017). Person Education. Harlow.
- Sparrow J. *The Culture Builders*. (2012). Gower Publishing Ltd. Surrey.

Chapter 6

Change

"The most effective way to manage change is to create it."
Peter Drucker (Author)

Introduction

It is impossible to escape change. You can move to Alaska and live in a wooden hut, but the ever-changing environment will still show you that change is unavoidable. In our personal lives and business lives, we experience change daily. On some days, we may want to scream out "stop changing while I catch up with the last change", but it will never stop. I emphasise this because not enough people are accepting that change is necessary and whether we want it or not, it is happening.

In recent years, change in business has been accelerating and this has been driven by technology. From the movement of business through bartering, to the exchanges of currency, the industrial revolution that brought steam power across the world as trains replaced horses, through to the modern-day explosion of the personal computer and internet. Every generation of leaders has dealt with transformational change on their watch. What makes change more pervasive is the increasing rapidity of change and the competitive advantage that can be gained or lost by the reaction to change.

The aim of this chapter is to help leaders understand their responsibilities as a role model in change. This chapter will look at change initiatives that have delivered both positive and negative outcomes and the learning that has occurred during this process. I will also focus on the requirement for leaders to speak up and not remain silent. This chapter will offer a combined change model based on the work of Lewin and Kotter to see how the two models can combine to help the delivery of change.

Planned vs unplanned change

My focus in this chapter is planned change. Where businesses have planned change, this change needs to be executed properly to ensure the benefits of the change are delivered. For bigger businesses, often with shareholders or Joint Venture Capital, change is heavily discussed and reported on at Board level. Where this affects the viability of the business, emergent change alone can seldom re-focus a business to a new stream of revenue or deliver medium to long-term competitive advantage. To stay competitive in a globalised market, with hyper competition from new entrants, substitutes or technological advances, change should be carefully assessed as a business case.

I have included in this chapter an assessment of models, case studies and guidance that is based on planned change. These discussion points may be useful when using other change models or when unplanned change occurs.

Leadership behaviour for change

Imagine you are sat in a meeting to discuss a future strategy and the leader asks for agreement before endorsing a specific way forward. What does it mean when you are silent at this point?

It is simple. If you choose not to speak up and air your concerns or alternative point of view, you have agreed with the proposed course of action. Even if you need to speak up and advise that the decision is rushed and you need to consider the proposals in more detail, do so. Too many leaders believe their silence is a protest or gives them the ability to not support the change initiative that is being taken forward. These actions are unsustainable behaviour in a business and should not be tolerated.

Now consider what silence means in a meeting when you have discussed a forthcoming change project. Along with the people who are silently disagreeing with you, there could be other factors at play in the room. Silence for some people can also mean other things:

- You have not explained yourself clearly.
- They are embarrassed to ask for further details thinking they should already know.
- There is a local or national custom which is preventing them from speaking out.
- This has been tried before but people are too polite to tell you.

If you have silent saboteurs within your ranks, call them out before you begin. Do not be afraid to open the discussion to establish if they are supporting and contributing the change, or against it. You need to know so you can adjust your stakeholder strategy. Challenging this behaviour at the outset will become more important when you progress through the stages of a change and start to consider building a project team, role models and making change stick.

Change models from Lewin & Kotter

As an MBA student I relished the opportunity to study change. I researched many different change models and enjoyed the differences between the models. But there were always two models that stood out for me; these were Lewin's 3-step model and Kotter's 8 stages. I connected with both and I have since used these models extensively to describe and support change through many organisations.

Leaders should be aware of some business models as much of the hard work has already been done as too many people want to start from what they consider is unique thinking. The key to using the models is interpretation and application to the situation that is experienced. I want to take a few moments to look at these two models in more detail and, how they fit with the current business environment despite their advancing age.

Kotter's 8 stage model

Kotter's eight stage model[60] is now 25 years old and still has value to the modern technology driven era. Here are the eight stages:

1. Establishing a sense of urgency.
2. Creating a guiding coalition.
3. Developing a vision and strategy.
4. Communicating the change vision.
5. Empowering employees for broad-based action.
6. Generating short-term wins.
7. Consolidating gains and producing more change.
8. Anchoring new approaches in the culture.

The longevity of this model is shown in Kotter's appreciation of the differences between the 20th century and 21st century. He identified an increase on the dependency of information systems coupled with reliance on more performance data which was supported by a shift in culture towards empowerment, openness and better decision making. In 'Leading Change' Kotter set out both why firms fail and the drivers of successful change. Building on Kotter's reasons why change fails and research from the Harvard Business Review[61] landmark study of change, here are an updated set of reasons to fail and some questions to ask to reduce the risk of failure.

1. Allow complacency
2. Lack of collaboration and coalition
3. Underestimate the power of vision
4. Under communicating the vision and purpose of the change
5. Permitting obstacles to block the new vision or purpose
6. Failing to create short-term wins
7. Declaring victory too soon
8. Neglecting to anchor changes in the corporate culture
9. Insufficient budget/time
10. Insufficient leadership

I will now provide a deeper explanation of each of these reasons.

Allow complacency

Complacency is present in every business. It does not matter if you have been listed in the top 10 Glassdoor 'best companies to work for'. Complacency exists. For many people this is borne out of the history of the company and how they have been led. Sitting in a comfort zone is great. There are no challenges, little stress, a person's knowledge is equal to or greater than the knowledge required to perform an activity and they do not have a leader pressing them to achieve more. Does this sound familiar? Unfortunately, it is leaders who allow complacency to exist and flourish. Protecting people from the realities of business, such as an understanding of the finances, competition or future direction, is a long-term issue. Complacency is best tackled through communication and openness.

- What can you share?
- How can people be involved and empowered?
- What action do you take when complacency continues?

Lack of collaboration and coalition

Change does not happen in a silo and work in isolation of other stakeholders because it is perceived that change can be delivered quicker is a recipe for resistance. Even though many see stakeholder engagement as a basic requirement for a change project, I have seen many efforts made to achieve inter-department changes without including the other departments. Delivering a solution to people that they have not been involved with and expecting them to simply adopt the change is naïve. Change gives an opportunity to reach out and build relationships around the business. There are opportunities here to identify key people who are the influencers in their department but not because of their title. They may be mentors to a collection of colleagues or simply have the respect that when they advocate for a project, others will listen.

- Who are the stakeholders?
- Who does the change affect?
- Who are they key influencers I need to engage?

Underestimate the power of vision

Vagueness is not the friend of change. Allowing people to form their own vision and then mis-communicate it with others is not how change is led. Without a clear vision, projects and initiatives are simply short-term activities that will quickly fade as one-week blends into another. A lack of vision will also make the commitment to the projects sparse and gatekeepers for the resources required to make the change successful will seldom release what is needed. Bringing people together and getting them to drive towards the same goal is only achieved through a clear powerful vision. Leaders can quickly use a vision to elevate their change initiative to a stronger position than previous attempts that may have gone un-noticed.

- What is your vision for the change?
- What benefits will this bring for the business?
- Have you tested your vision for understanding?

Under communicating the vision and purpose of the change

Communication is not achieved in an email. Lack of communication within a change project is the opportunity for immediate failure as employees lose faith in what is trying to be achieved as key leaders are invisible. The vision for change is not a one-off email that is never referred to again and the purpose cannot be a complex tome that few have the time to read and comprehend. For the vision and purpose to be understood, they should be clear, concise and available to everyone. Meaningful communication is achieved by the presence and clear involvement of leaders and influencers throughout the business who can openly champion the work that is being proposed and easily explain the benefits.

- What is your 2-minute elevator pitch for your change? This is a succinct explanation that can be given on a regular basis to a few people or large groups when reinforcing the need for change.
- Who are the key leaders/influencers that need to be part of the messaging?
- How will this be communicated to people and how often will this be reinforced?

Permitting obstacles to block the new vision or purpose

People, processes and technology are all potential obstacles to achieving your new vision. The most powerful obstacle are people, and these must be dealt with directly and swiftly. Just as change will fail if stakeholders and influencers are not engaged in the processes, people may take more direct action to block change to protect their position or beliefs about how the business should operate. Processes and technology can be quicker to change but the detail of the changes may take longer to establish when they are inter-woven with other business practices. Regardless of the source of the obstacle, as a leader you are there to overcome the obstacles and communicate continually with people to dispel any myths that the project cannot continue.

- Who/what are the blockers to this change?
- How can these blockers be removed?

- How can I re-communicate that any obstacles have been removed?

Failing to create short-term wins

You cannot eat an elephant in one bite. Taking a vision and creating one massive plan including all stakeholders across the business which may span 1-2 years is undeliverable. Employees cannot see their contribution let alone the positive outcome until the whole project is delivered. Gatekeepers cannot see how/when their resource is being used, other than for the whole project, and are unlikely to get behind an unwieldy project.

The art of short-term wins is for people to see how they are delivering the desired aim and that progress is being made. Kotter was clear that the emphasis is on creating short-term wins and not simply assuming or hoping they will occur. Short-term wins can be achieved by breaking the change project into phases with deliverables for each phase. The resources needed for each phase need to be clearly articulated and it is important to make sure that stakeholders are part of the 'win' moment so they remain committed to the overall project.

- How can you arrange your change project into a series of smaller, connected projects?
- What success criteria will determine that a 'win' has been achieved?
- How can you celebrate often without drawing people away from the project?

Declaring victory too soon

Only say it is done when it is done. People are fickle and will want to move onto the next project as soon as possible, especially if it is more interesting than your change project. The pressure is felt by both leader and employee to deliver the current project and then start to deliver the next one. Businesses often fail to realise the benefits of their expensive change projects as other pressures have already built up to deliver new changes. Leaders must be careful to avoid the pressure to declare victory before it is genuinely in place because as soon as this is done, there is little chance of re-visiting the project to finish off the remaining items. This is a test of courage for a leader who must not be distracted by the pressures to declare victory.

- What are the success criteria for the project?
- Who determines victory?
- Who do I need to influence to ensure that victory is not declared without my agreement?

Neglecting to anchor changes in the corporate culture

Change is not real change until it is part of the culture. Some people will continue to avoid change until it is so rooted in the culture of the organisation that they cannot function without adopting the change. The behaviours and attitudes of employees and leaders are the outcomes of change, which should drive greater performance. Change is not a one-time action. Constant affirmation of the change and reflection that the change has led to a better performance are the ways this can be fixed into the culture. An email to tell people of a change of culture is not sustainable change, no matter who it is sent from. Leaders who are aware of the cultural challenge from the outset will achieve more than leaders who try to ignore the level of challenge.

The implementation of change can be further enhanced by a full understanding of how the current culture has evolved and the business history.

- How did our culture evolve to where it is today?
- What are the main indicators that culture has changed in our business?
- Who are the role models that others will look up to for cultural cues?

Insufficient budget/time

Cheaper and faster can often mean more work and cost later. How serious are you and your business about a change project? Real change can only be achieved when the business commits to the endeavour through people, provide resources and are realistic about the time it will take. One of the greatest challenges is for business to run a change project using people within their business who already have an operational target to deliver.

This creates a dichotomy between the normal now and the future normal which many people find impossible to deliver. The change challenge is compounded when the changes will directly affect the people asked to deliver the change. Even just a few select people who are engaged on a short-term basis can create the core of a project team to bring together others to deliver a successful project. The benefits of previous experience and a healthy level of distance from the impact of the outcomes (i.e. a specific project team) can deliver a project with a greater likelihood of success. Consider these questions for implementing change:

- Will the business make more resources available to support the project?
- What is the timeline for delivery and is this realistic for meaningful change?

- What level of influence do I have in seeking and agreeing realistic resources?

Insufficient leadership

If you must ask who the leader is, stop the project. Leaders need to be visible throughout a project and not lurk in the shadows. I worked on a change programme where the Director of the department sat in the back of meetings, making the odd note of our discussions, whilst I worked with his team to deliver a change project across many locations with 3000 people. His focus and effort were towards transactional and lower-level tasks, such as booking lunch and taking out the remains of lunch to the kitchen, instead of providing strategic direction that his team needed. It was clear to me that his deputy was the real leader who showed courage, calmness and gave a sense of direction to the stakeholders sat around the table. Visitors to the project office would often ask about the Director, who was the sponsor of the project, and what his role was. If you are leading a change project, it is your responsibility to be bold and be present. If there is no clear leader of a project or too many leaders causing confusion, you have a duty to ask for clarity on the leader. Consider these points for a project you are involved with:

- Who is the leader of the change project?
- What are the indicators that you are providing good leadership for the project?
- What can the business learn from your leadership of the change project?

Lewin's 3-step model

Lewin's original research was around social conflict and how behavioural change could be achieved. His work included studies on field theory, group dynamics and action research along with his 3-step model for organisational change (Burns 2004[62]). Lewin believed that successful change included 3 steps: unfreezing, moving and refreezing. This model has been reviewed on many occasions by many people who have sought to add extra steps to his model. However, I have provided a short summary of this model together with a modern application to businesses:

Step 1 – Unfreezing

You cannot make an omelette without cracking eggs. The difficult part of change is for people to unlearn their old behaviours before new ones can be adopted.
The work required is not simply asking people to change but helping them to understand the reason for the change and what it means for them. Some people will still be trying to accept the

previous change when unfreezing once again commences but will quickly announce that the current status quo works fine. A quick turnaround from the previous week of resisting the previous change! It is this potential for loss that will cause resistance and this must be overcome through discussion and understanding before the old behaviours can be let go.

Step 2 – Moving

Moving to a new state is an iterative process. Leaders need to learn about the forces impacting upon change from the unfreezing step to establish the new set of behaviours. It is impossible to define a new set of behaviours and then simply hand these back to the people who are at the forefront of the change project. The new behaviours need to be continually assessed, amended and repeated. At this point, the stickiness of the change will need to be reinforced by the leader(s) to prevent slippage back to old behaviours.

Step 3 – Re-freezing

Backwards is not moving forwards. For the change to stick, Lewin saw this as a group activity which delivered stability for the new behaviours. Change can only be made permanent once it is part of the culture of the business and not seen as the new fad that will pass easily. Role modelling the behaviours throughout the business whilst addressing the policies and other symbols of the business are necessary for change to stick.

Change model for leaders

In 2017 I brought Kotter's 8 stages and Lewin's 3-step model together to celebrate the models and define a new change model based on these classics (Figure 6.1). I have amended the headings slightly to make the 3 steps more aligned with the surrounding actions and changed the titles of the steps to give more explanation in business terms. These amendments now give a framework of change:

- Change readiness – Businesses need to be aware of what they are working with before embarking on change. Assuming that people, processes and technology are ready and able to handle change is a key point of failure. Preliminary work is required before launching the project.

- Change takes root – You can use whatever metaphor you wish at this point to describe the start of something new. Once you see those 'buds' or 'green shoots' it is time to do something with them.

- Embedding the change – By now, leaders are often looking towards the next change project but this is the key moment to ensure there is no backward slippage.

I have refined Kotter's 8 stages and I now have 7 stages which give a more consumable model to leaders who wish to adopt the model, apply timelines and the outcomes of their change project for further discussion with stakeholders.

The 'Change model for leaders' was originally designed to support the implementation of HR systems and was based on the need to deliver a project and then embed the outcomes for the medium to long-term. The 'Change model for leaders' now has the following supporting stages:

- **Create a sense of urgency** – The need to change must be understood. Is this about business survival? Are we operating a system that is de-supported that now needs to be replaced? Have our competition gained first-mover advantage in a new market? There are many more reasons for change on a macro or micro scale but regardless of this scale, there must be an understanding of why change is needed to bring people to the discussion.

- **Create the vision** – The need for a clear vision, which is easily understood, is paramount and will be used throughout the course of the project. The vision should be focussed on the benefits that will be realised from the project (cost savings, business survival, process improvements, opening of markets etc.) Considerable effort should be expended to refine this simple statement and then to continually communicate the vision in every stage of the project. Establishing a vision exposes the need for clear communications to all stakeholders and the need for expert communications support.

- **Build the project team** – Can you really deliver a change project whilst delivering your day job? Probably not. Leaders need to assess properly the capacity and capability of a team to understand how the project will be resourced with the right people. The establishment of the project team can lead to a hybrid approach of internal and external people but the project will seldom work with solely internal people who have been asked to do more work. The project team may grow and shrink at different times of the project but a strong core who are dedicated to achieving the vision can accommodate transient members of the group.

Figure 6.1 - Change model for leaders

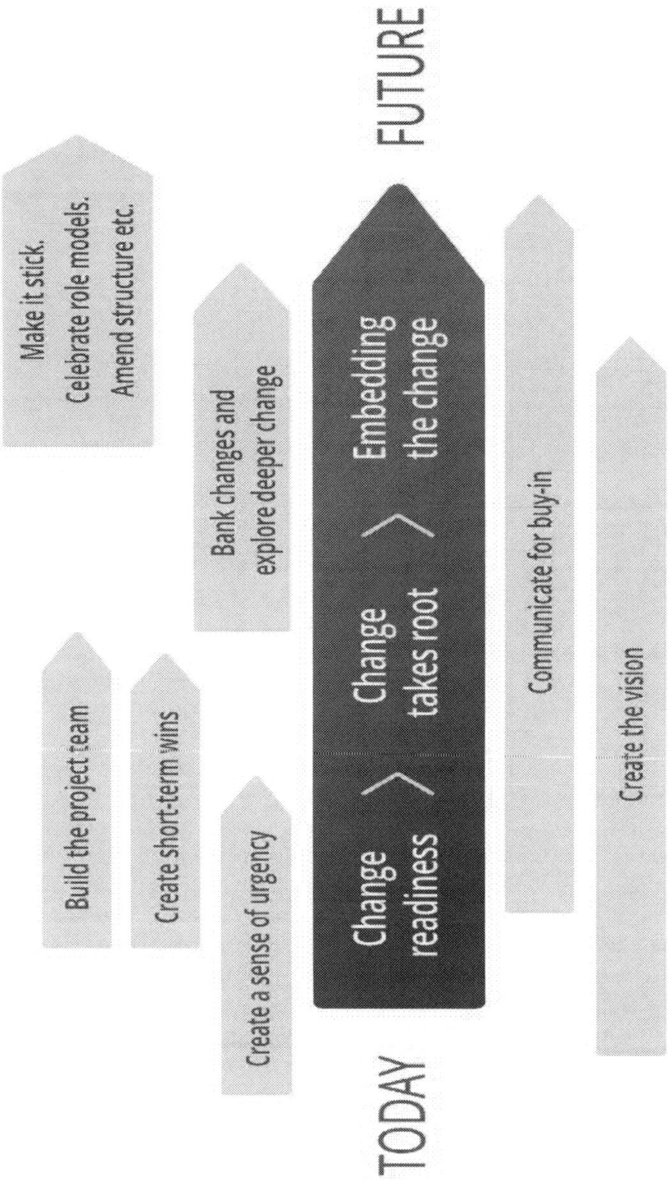

- (continued) As the complexity and scale of projects increase, a responsible leader who is committed to achieving the vision should be realistic about how the project will be delivered. The make-up of the project team and the progress they are making should be under constant review with the leader ready to make tweaks to the team during the project lifecycle.

- **Create short-terms wins** – This is the time to create some noise and draw on the communications support to tell stakeholders of the progress and early success. These wins make the changes real for the project team and ensures that everyone involved is the change. Short-term wins are about motivation. By starting to deliver on the vision, even in small chunks, you will be able to unsettle the resistors to change and embolden the role models of change. Plan these short-term wins into the project from the outset but don't go too far in letting the project focus on short-term wins at the expense of achieving the overall vision. There needs to be a balance.

- **Communicate for buy-in** – You cannot do too much communication of the need for change, the vision, short-terms wins, role models etc. It is paramount there must be a well thought out communication strategy that is central to the project and not an afterthought. Th communications strategy needs its own leader who is wedded to the project team. Communications should start early, be consistent throughout the project, and then continue after the formal project has concluded until it has become part of the fabric of the business.

- **Bank changes and explore deeper change** – Once the change project starts to deliver some changes, they need to be recognised, communicated and reinforced throughout the business. It is the reinforcement or 'banking' that requires the most attention as it is too easy for the initial changes to slip and previous processes to re-surface. Some simple acts of recognition can help cement the change through public appreciation, personal notes of thanks or use of an employee reward scheme. Banked changes are truly reinforced when the person leading the change then acts as a role model for others including mentoring colleagues to adopt changes in their team or department.

- **Make it stick** – This is the point at which the change becomes business as usual. This occasion may be signified by a change of location, people, processes or technology. It could be through a customer launch that is only possible with the changes that have been made. Even a change to the businesses mission statement or reflected in KPIs (Key performance indicators) for senior executives that has not been possible before the change has been completed. The leader will know when it has truly been made to stick because people will refer to it as the 'old' model and will talk about future changes they wish to make.

Change failure

To help understand how a change project can go wrong, I have provided a brief explanation of how an impactful change project failed. When you are reading this recollection of events, please consider the 10 reasons for failure highlighted previously in the chapter and see if you can identify where this change failed.

During an audit of a HR division, I spoke to the HR Director with many years of experience as a leader of change. He was a friend of my boss and the pressure was on me to deliver a great audit report from this site. The HRD and his team looked after a wide collection of people and part of the site was a college. Young trainees would arrive and spend 12-16 weeks learning their trade before securing permanent positions around the country. The college had experienced some issues with a drinking culture that had led to challenges with the younger learners.

The HRD had personally led a review into the care and social provision for the learners and had concluded that a separate area in the social club was needed to offer a space away from alcoholic drinks. The students could still access soft drink and snacks through a hatch, away from the more boisterous members of the social club. The HRD had partnered with several organisations and gained funding to make the new social environment an appealing place for the students and it opened to a great fanfare. Having heard so much about this before my visit, and during the initial meeting with the HRD, I made a point of visiting the social club to see the impact he had made.

It really was a great space for people to relax, unwind and some amazing facilities. I could see why he was proud of this project. I saw the social club manager and I wanted to get her view on the changes that had been made. Just like everyone else, she spoke highly of the project which was designed to protect vulnerable young people. I asked about the hatch where the students could buy soft drink and snacks. That was the moment people around me took a deep breath.

Without hesitation, the social club manager told me they do not really open the hatch as it's a distraction for the person working at the bar on the other side. Her and the bar team all found it easier if the students go into the bar and then carry their purchases back into their community space. I was shocked that the entire project had just been compromised and other people knew about this. When I gathered my thoughts, I asked how long this had been the case.

The social club manager said that after a week they closed the hatch. She did not see anything wrong with this and when I discussed the project aims and advised that a lot of investment had been put into this venture, she simply shrugged her shoulders.

I was gutted for the HRD. I was also frustrated that the HRD had not followed up to make the change stick. He had forgotten the basics and especially the feedback loop. It was an incredibly difficult debriefing session. He had been let down and as the leader of the project, he was accountable. The showpiece project for others to follow would take another 12 months before he could measure the impact as he had to re-start his project and embed the changes properly.

Case Study - Leading Change and Transformation: 5 Lessons from the Frontlines

Deborah Hartung, Founder of Personify Change Ltd, deborah-hartung.com

Working as an independent management consultant for almost 14 years now, I have had the privilege of working on many different projects and being appointed to various senior interim roles – including a couple of multi-million-dollar projects with one of the global "big 4" management consultancies.

The clients and projects are always varied and interesting and I never come away from these engagements without having made new friends or having learned all manner of business and leadership lessons.

The most challenging engagement by far, was what should have been a pretty straightforward digital transformation and HR technology deployment with a NYSE listed company with over 30 000 employees, globally. Quite surprisingly for most people, it was not the scale or the geography that derailed this one… instead, as I have learned countless times, in the end, it came down to leadership and organizational culture. Simply put, this project was a nightmare across all work streams.

Since I specialize in the human change and organizational transformation aspects though, let us focus our attention on the top 5 lessons on leading change in the new world of work:

Case for Change vs Reason for Change

As part of any project within any organisation, there has to be a compelling "business case" to justify the project and the associated expenses. Across the board, these are pretty standard, with a definitive commercial or P&L bias and very detailed cost/benefit analyses.

A business case will usually outline the background facts before explaining the expected business benefits, the various options considered (with reasons for rejecting or recommending each possible option or course of action), the expected project costs and the various risks associated with maintaining the status quo versus moving forward with the proposed project. A typical business case, therefore, details and summarizes:

- *Reasons;*
- *Options;*
- *Benefits;*
- *Costs;*
- *Timescales and*
- *Risk.*

All of this is crucial information that helps business leaders determine which projects to prioritize and to properly plan the allocation of funds and internal resources. So, we see a lot of "burning platform" narratives or focus on cost savings or some improvements in efficiency for the company. This is important to senior leaders and shareholders. But, in the end, it is not a "business case" that will motivate people to change their ways of working or to adopt new processes or technology. Employees at all levels throughout the organisation want an answer to one simple question: What is in it for me (WIIFM)?

Telling the stories of WIIFM create powerful narratives around the "reason for change" and these, in turn, create positive momentum and a desire to change, across the board. Crucial to selling the WIIFM, of course, is truly understanding the different stakeholders and their pain points and then tailoring the narrative and message towards those stakeholders. Which brings me to my next lesson.

Change is a Marketing Exercise

No matter how you try and slice it, organisational change management is a marketing exercise and needs marketing expertise in addition to the typical change models we all know and love. Marketing professionals have a proven track record of changing hearts and minds and telling compelling stories around the WIIFM.
Any change project worth its salt these days, will have spent significant time on identifying the "North Star" message and building a lexicon of words and phrases that support that messaging so that all communications are tailored towards the specific stakeholder group (target audience). Doing this work up-front, before embarking on any

other change activities is one of the single most effective means of ensuring that change will be well-received and embedded within the organisation. Focus on truly understanding the different personas and invest in some UX design aspects as you deploy communications and change interventions.

Change Impacts Culture – Always

Sure, you can do your Change Impact Analysis and create heat maps and whatever other fun tools you might want to use. But if you think for one second that a change project is NOT going to have an impact on workplace culture, you would be sorely mistaken and you would ignore culture impact at your own peril.
When we deploy new technology or ways of working as we often find ourselves doing these days, we are challenging the status quo on many levels that are not immediately visible. Often, we are challenging people's very idea of their role and their authority and how they fit into the bigger picture. We might be creating transparency and autonomy for the most junior employees in a very hierarchical workplace where phrases like "need to know" or "above your pay grade" are still widely used. Imagine for a moment the seismic power shift that occurs in an environment like that! Suddenly employees at all levels have access to information and they have the ability to influence and control their personal career development, instead of being dependent on their line managers.

Managers can update an organogram or flag a vacancy and it is no longer "HR's job". All of these changes have big impacts on the people working in an organisation. It is not just about possible organizational efficiency or restructures - it is about their way of being at work and how they relate to others and how they see themselves and their autonomy and authority – and that makes it a workplace culture impact.

Culture Impacts Change

Most organisations I have worked with, are blissfully unaware of what their true workplace culture really is. They have their core values emblazoned on every wall possible and they genuinely believe they are doing a great job. But the core values and the ping pong tables and the cold brew coffee is all just smoke and mirrors and all speaks to an aspirational culture that – in my experience – hardly ever exists in any workplace.

The true workplace culture can be found in the organizational structures and the ways of working. It is "the way we do things around here". The core values poster may say "equality", but hierarchies reign supreme and most employees would not recognize any member of the C-Suite if they were standing next to them in an elevator. Similarly, a core value of "teamwork" might be overshadowed by the very real competition instead of collaboration, happening on the ground.

Change projects have a better chance of success if you are realistic about your true workplace culture and the behaviours within the Organization, instead of making assumptions about the core values and aspirational culture. Build your change strategy, plans, messaging and interventions around the true culture and work with "what is" instead of "what we wish we had".

Choose the Right Change Team

This one is not going to win me any new fans amongst the broader HR and OCM (Organisational Change Management) community, but I would be doing you a disservice if I did not point out that sometimes it is the change team themselves who sink projects before they have even started. I have worked with loads of different types of people and in my experience, it is a recipe for disaster to have a cautious, highly introverted "completer finisher" type of person as a Change Lead as they are likely to get caught up in process and details and they themselves find it hard to deviate from their change management handbook from 1987.

As with any project team, you need a balance of personalities, skills and role preferences. Most importantly though, you need a visionary, enthusiastic, collaborative, empathetic and extroverted individual at the helm, as they are more likely to see the bigger picture and be able to read between the lines and take different stakeholder needs and perspectives into account.

On the project in question, the client's culture was extremely conservative, hierarchical and safety driven. They had invested millions of dollars in procuring the best-in-class HR Technology that would absolutely revolutionize their ways of working and flip the balance of power for many transactional tasks, solidly into the hands of their employees.

The company failed or refused to acknowledge their cautious and conservative culture or the impact this would have on the pace of change and the adoption of new ways of working. They also ignored the culture impacts, despite being made aware of these through a custom-built expanded change impact analysis.

Needless to say, trying to sell the "burning platform" business case fell horribly flat in every stakeholder engagement session and the project was very much doomed from the start. Two years later, long after they had booted our fancy team of consultants and ignored at least 90% of our advice, they finally managed to deploy the new HR system to much confusion and controversy and without even a 40% user adoption rate.

All of these challenges could have been avoided on this project if the five simple lessons I have shared, were applied. Fortunately, I have had the privilege - along with many other consultants and business leaders just like me - of learning from countless mistakes.

I have spoken to Deborah about her case study on many occasions and we still identify new lessons each time with talk about how poor leadership affected the example project. What remains a clearly obvious failure is the business decided to bring change experts into the project and then not support them. This is a business who were interested in the outcomes of the project but were clearly not dependant on the success of the project.

Leading change

We can all learn from colleagues and friends on how they have successfully led change. It is not a rite of passage to get it wrong and then learn from it. Change affects the personal lives of people and should be handled with care, precision and empathy for those who are affected. Leaders will always approach the change in many ways but it is useful to hear from some great examples. I spoke with a senior executive from a technology business who explained how he led a complex change programme which saw a business teetering on the edge of collapse.

> *"I got parachuted in the day that I had to start the plan of sorting it out and meet all the people. Because I didn't have any a prior knowledge or expertise in that business, you just have to focus on some real fundamentals. Sometimes that makes it so clear. There were some good people, there was some amazing customer relations. There was a massive opportunity in this specific sector. Their commercial model, their cash flow profile, the volume of products that they were attempting to support but the way in which they were marketing the value of this solution and the way it's being received in terms of its perception of value was just horrific. The business was about to close.*
>
> *Within the first hour, I had to address all the staff, so they knew there was a problem. They knew it was an absolute fundamental problem.*
>
> *So, I thought, well, let's get everybody together. And, we weren't going to have an open debate as such, we're definitely going to have questions and it was just this is what's going on. This is what we need to do. You need to give me sufficient time*

to assimilate the information and I will come back to you within the next two weeks.

In the meantime, I'm going to give you a daily brief briefing of that position and where we go next. I think getting a combination of the managers and key people in, we obviously spoke to all the staff in terms of daily briefings, but within the first two weeks, we got most of the staff to get their views and their understanding. And I think that's the point I'm making is often these programmes are pre-emptively done, and you actually miss out on the opportunity of actually uncovering huge opportunities and avoiding a huge calamity. So, this was an ugly situation that we had to correct. In the first few weeks, we got a plan.

What are two things that I'll draw out of this? We anticipated that we're going to have to communicate really and be able to be able to evidence the actions that we were taking. And that that would mean that at the point, we got it back on an even keel and things, we started to think about diminishing the communication that could create a vacuum. That could create perception that we've stopped communicating, which is worrying. So how do we transition to normal or let people know it's a positive thing? We are going to have to lose some people. So, we were absolutely on how do we get the message right? And really managing the survivors.

It was six tough months. But we got the businesses healthy. We just completely converted, how they did their revenue model and they've rationalised the products and got it good. The point I'm making here and what it taught me was to two main things. It taught me that you have to think about the way in which you work with those people for the solution in that crisis event.

One of the main people I work with said to them, 'why wouldn't we just manage businesses like this the whole time'? I don't mean the crisis; I mean the consultative approach. Once you've got a set of these tools, you can pretty much go into any business and I think this is the real value of consultants. You can actually pinpoint the fundamentals incredibly quickly, because you've not got the burden of either being too close to the problem or all of the baggage of the past."

I have talked to the leader about this project on a few occasions and the main point of his story is the amount of communication with the people in that business. The leader tackled this head on within the first hour and continued that throughout his time leading that business.

As a leader, it is this ability to seize the moment, be confident and communicate clearly with people around you. He did this incredibly well, bringing the people in the business along on the journey and making them aware of the situation they were experiencing. His transparent approach to leadership coupled with clear communication should serve as an example of how change can be led.

This example of change was driven by a clear need in the business; we either change or close. My great friend and leadership consultant Hiten Bhatt explained on my podcast that he has a slightly different explanation for the reason people want to make a change stick:

> *"In the Shawshank Redemption, the plotline is innocent man gets accused of killing his wife. He didn't kill his wife. He's put in this horrible prison. And he escaped from that prison. And by the end of the movie, he's on this beach. I often use this analogy when I'm talking about change. At the end of the movie, he's where he wants to be, which is on the beach. But to escape, there's a scene in the movie where he has to tunnel through miles of sewage to get to that beach and to escape. Basically, why change fails is because change is tough. There's going to be a load of shit involved. He really struck on a fundamental path of that standard deviation curve of humans and how they act a large amount of people. The reason people don't save for retirement and the reason people eat the extra cream bun when they're trying to lose weight, is because they can't quite get the vision of what the results would be if they didn't do that. They did something else, projecting into the future. So, you've got to set that future vision and make it really compelling to put the effort into getting to that journey."*

Hiten is highlighting the need for a clear vision for people to focus on and to see the outcomes that will be achieved once a demanding process has been completed. The number of projects that are started but abandoned because of lack of belief in the outcomes or that people were not prepared for such a tough ride will never be calculated – but the number is high!

Survivor syndrome

Change does not stop the minute you have declared the change project to have been completed. In fact, this is just the beginning of the next phase of change which is the normalisation of that change into the business.

The starting point here is the people who have been affected by the change and how they are feeling. Woodward and Buchholz[63] identified four reactions to change including disengagement (withdrawal), disidentification (sadness/worry), disorientation (confusion) and disenchantment (anger). These four reactions are a simple categorisation of how people will be feeling after a change has taken place and below is a summary showing the behaviours of the four reactions:

Figure 6.2 – 4 reactions to change

Disengagement	Disidentification	Disorientation	Disenchantment
• Being hard to find • Doing only the basic requirements • Shrugging shoulders • Will not ask questions • Will not seek information • Will not discuss with others	• Reminiscing • Sulking • Dwelling on the past • Continuing to do the old job • Associating with the previous work team • Resisting new procedures	• Always ask questions • Does the wrong things • Gets others to ask questions • May worry or even 'catastrophize' • Becomes very detail orientated • Involves others in the questioning process • Does not know the priorities • Leaves work undone until questions are answered	• Raised, intense tone of voice • Walks out • Refuses to talk • Shows self-pity • Tries to get others on their side • Backstabbing • Sabotage

The 'Reactions to change' framework gives a detailed assessment of which reaction the employee will be experiencing and will require a range of actions to tackle the behaviours. As a leader you should understand the impact of change across your team, especially where the change has resulted in the movement/redundancy of people.

The people that remain after the change project is completed should be your immediate concern as they could be feeling some element of 'survivor syndrome'[64] which brings together these 4 reactions. Survivor Syndrome is often experienced in businesses where change has taken place, long serving people have left, and the remaining staff struggle to deal with the loss of their colleagues.

An important factor that is often underestimated is the way the leavers were dealt with during the process. If 'survivors' see that people were dealt with fairly, financially compensated, treated with dignity and supported through CV workshops/resettlement schemes, this can lessen the impact on the survivors. The achievements and contributions of the leavers should be celebrated so they can reflect on their time with the business. A strong culture has a series of myths and stories associated with both current and former employees. By nurturing these stories so people can see they have a place in the corporate history makes an ever-lasting connection and survivors can positively remember their former colleagues.

However, survivors often feel isolated, abandoned and question 'why wasn't I selected to leave?'. If these thoughts go unchecked, the likelihood of turnover of the remaining people will increase. For businesses who have reacted to a shift in the marketplace or the introduction of new technology which now needs fewer people, the risk of keeping the valued people who survived the restructuring should be a real concern. Leaders should be working closely with their HR teams and ask if the business has an Employment Assistance Programme that includes counselling. Survivors can then access professional support, outside of the workplace, to help work through their reactions. This support is further evidence of the way the change has taken place for both the leavers and survivors and helps people understand that the business cares for survivors and their future.

You have an opportunity to lead people into the future and not let them dwell. You can do this through a variety of activities but the real key is communication. This includes celebrating the achievements of the people who have moved on, visioning a new future and setting targets that focus on the strengths of the remaining people.

As a leader, you should be accessible to people and make space for open conversations. Restructuring and redundancy is part of the history of the business and will not be forgotten. Do not try to ignore that it happened. Acknowledge it and look to the future. Have you spoken to any of your leavers after they have left? Even by chance in the pub? Celebrate how people are getting on. For people who may be suffering survivor's syndrome, this will help to understand that there is a positive outcome to a restructure or merger.

Role models

Who are your leadership role models? I asked this question during my podcast and got a variety of answers including parents, business leaders, religious leaders and academics. The reasons the guests saw them as role models was more enlightening than the people they had selected. They talked about key traits such as empathy, dignity, humbleness, humility and kindness that had been shown by their role models and how they had learnt from them.

We may not realise it, but at different times of our lives we have different roles models and we learn from each one. It is impossible to underestimate the presence of role models during a change project. They are the spark for your fire and you should aim to identify role models quickly so you can build part of the project around them.

It is not about a title. Role models for change are not the ones with the most senior title. Role models are the people who buy-in to the vision and see the possible outcomes. They live the change project and talk freely about the benefits this will bring or has already brought to their team. You should spend time with your role models to ensure they remain with you on the journey and see how comfortable they are at telling their story to other people through articles, townhalls, webinars, videos or any other communication method you can access to get your message to your audience. Make sure they are accessible to the people you are trying to convince. You may run an online seminar with a Q&A session, but some people will want to directly approach your role models to test their thoughts about the change project and understand if this is real or just corporate nonsense.

Role models need to be authentic and it is not something that you can force on someone. Your wider stakeholders will sniff out an actor and this will damage the credibility of the change project. If you are struggling to find role models, you need to go back and review the vision for the project and your intended outcomes. If you really cannot find anyone that is willing to talk about and promote the change you are trying to make, why are you doing it?

Summary

Change requires effort. Not just superficial effort or an initial push but meaningful effort on a daily basis. My favourite of all the failures discussed above is 'declaring victory too early'. It is an easy mistake to commit as a busy leader who is trying hard to impress. Declaring victory too early and rushing to start the next project that demands your attention will simply lead to the first project taking longer and not sticking (delivering the results that were expected). And throughout all the change activities you lead, remember that at the heart of change are people. The people affected by change need clear communication, early role models and confidence that the vision is achievable.

Reflective activities

- Think of a change you were involved in recently. Was it planned or unplanned? Was there a clear vision that was set out to all stakeholders? What level of communication existed throughout the project? Did the project achieve the desired outcomes? Did this result in survivor syndrome? Who were the role models in this change? How would you improve on this change project if you ran it again?

- Think of the best change project you have been involved with. What made it great? Who were the leaders and why did they standout? What can you take from them into your next project?

Suggested reading

- Hodges J. (2017). *Consultancy, Organizational Development and Change*. London: Kogan Page.
- Hodges J. (2021). *Managing and Leading People through Organizational Change*. London: Kogan Page.
- Arussy L. (2018). *Next is Now, 5 steps for embracing change*. New York: Simon & Schuster.

Chapter 7

Customer driven leadership

"I think of customer service as an offence and not a defence."
Gary Vaynerchuk (Chairman of VaynerX)

Introduction

When was the last time you experienced fantastic customer service? Not just the superficial 'have a nice day' but real, deep-seated customer service that you feel ran through a business and their products or services? Now ask yourself, how did that make you feel when you had that experience? I expect that you may have identified one example of great customer service quickly but what if I asked you to do it again now? I suspect it would be a lot harder because the customer service you thought of initially remains with you because it is so infrequent.

Businesses that have customer service at their core, and is instilled into every employee, are few. They operate in a space many can only aspire to reach and this is often driven by an associated cost to the customer. A 7-star hotel is an example of this type of customer service.

This dedication to service, excellence and concentration on the finest of details is what makes the difference, all of this starts with the leaders. It cascades from the General Manager through the business and is represented by each subsequent layer of leadership.

Some of the US airlines (Delta and Southwest) have been held up as great examples of customer service with incredible stories of people going beyond expectations to resolve issues for passengers. But these same airlines have been subject to massive changes in the industry and several acquisitions which have lessened the once enviable stories of service.

Some years ago, I was speaking to a CEO about his ongoing battle with poor customer service throughout the business. He had stood up in front of town halls, sent out emails and put posters on the walls. He had done everything he could think of to communicate to people about how to improve their customer service. He explained that the biggest impact he had was not through any of those traditional communication channels. It was the act of him going and spending an hour a day listening to calls via the customer support phone lines.

Through speaking to the customers, listening to the customers, understanding the challenges of both the customer and the support person, he realised that he needed to make improvements within the support structure itself. That led back to where the sales were made. He took these actions years before other people had taken the boss back to the floor. It was enlightening listening to a leader who had about 1000 people in his organisation and who had taken customer calls for an hour a day. He spoke to his employees about what he had learned from this experience. When they heard of his calls with the customers, the impact was tenfold.

In this chapter, I will look deeper into customer driven leadership that delivers better business outcomes. Importantly, this will consider research to establish the demands of customers and how leaders can align their strategy to meet the needs of a more informed and digitally savvy customer who has access to a global marketplace.

Better business outcomes

Why do we need to have any focus on customer service? The reputation of a business will rely on great customer service which is now easily rated using apps and online reviews. Warren Buffet, US business magnate, investor and philanthropist said "It takes 20 years to build a reputation and five minutes to ruin it. If you think about that, you'll do things differently." Any leader who is not worried about their business reputation or the impact that their customer focus has on their business will not last long. Many businesses rely heavily on return customers and can be easily affected by poor ratings. A study by Dimensional Research[65] identified that 54% of people tell at least five other people about a bad experience with a business. Whilst most people will expect that negative experiences will gain more coverage than positive experiences, what is striking from the research is that 58% of people are more likely to tell others about their customer experience today than they would have five years ago. This increase in sharing of the customer experience has its roots in the availability of social media and the research also shows that people are more likely to share negative experiences than positive ones.

As leaders, you should consider what business outcomes are achieved through better customer service. Every business is different and so are your challenges, products and services, so it's important that you consider the context in which you are working. The following statistics from research undertaken by Superoffice[66],based on a survey of nearly 2000 businesses, provides more reasons to consider your customer driven leadership:

- 45.9% of business said that customer experience is their top priority in the next five years.

- 86% of buyers are willing to pay more for a great customer experience.

- More than two-thirds of companies now compete primarily based on customer experience.
- 57% of customers won't recommend a business with a poorly designed website on mobile.
- 44% will increase the investment in their customer experience initiatives in the next year.

But what about empowerment? Empowering frontline staff to make decisions without a complex escalation procedure does two things. Firstly, it makes your people feel valued and trusted. Secondly, they will be more engaged in the customer experience and are more likely to go the extra mile for the customer and the business. The starting point for customer driven leadership is your own people and focusing on supporting them to be able to do their job. The better they can do this, with the least amount of friction, the better the customer service they will provide. Most people want to give their best and be professional in doing their job. If you think about a time when you have been unable to do a job because of a lack of trust, resources, processes or a lack of direction, how did you feel? If you're unable to perform in your role, you are likely to suffer from stress and become more likely to leave.

I mentioned the ability of hotels to deliver incredible customer service and the Ritz-Carlton is one such example. I've had the pleasure of staying in their hotels around the world and the level of service is an experience. John R. DiJulius[67] is known for his work in the field of customer service and has written an excellent book, *'What's the Secret?: To Providing a World-Class Customer Experience'*, about customer experience. After a stay in the Ritz-Carlton, Sarasota, he accidentally left his laptop charger in the room.

He arrived home and before he could call the hotel to discuss the missing charger, he received a delivery of a new charger – courtesy of the hotel. This gesture was completed by the Ritz-Carlton under their '2000' rule where employees are empowered to remedy an issue for a customer up to the value of $2000 per incident. This customer service is an example of a business using a problem for a customer as a way of delivering a great customer service experience. This example is well used throughout blogs, podcasts and webpages to show how personalised customer service can be delivered.

Customer driven leaders not only create a climate where their people can excel at their jobs but they also deliver phenomenal customer service. The business outcomes of this culture are a better business through a revered reputation, standing and repeat business within the industry. Another direct impact of not delivering customer driven leadership is the turnover of good people.

If your employees are ashamed of the service you provide and have to deal with the backlash from your customers, they will leave. This becomes an ever-worsening problem as it then becomes harder to attract top staff who do not wish to be associated with a business that is known for poor customer service.

When customer driven leadership goes wrong

The speed of the internet enables swift communication with customers about offers, product recalls, tips for using products, competitions and general marketing. Together with social media, customers now have access to a broader range of products and services than ever before as they can now shop across the globe. The same technology has also been used by customers to highlight issues and give feedback. The speed and directness of this feedback can help to resolve issues but also shine a light on poor practices. In May 2021, one of my network tweeted the following:

> *So shopping, I ask assistant where the fuses are, " no idea- not my patch", I say, can you ask someone?, answer came back " no if you stand there long enough someone might come along"!! Really what crap service!!! So dissatisfied with this customer service!!!!*

In 261 characters, she has communicated with the business, given a summary of the negative interaction and provided her assessment of their customer service. There was no requirement to provide a detailed letter to a manager or ask for a feedback form which then had to be laboriously completed (a practice proven to deter would-be complainants). This is in the public domain the second my contact shared the tweet. This retailer now has an opportunity to engage with her directly through DMs to provide an apology and identify the store to they can pass the feedback to the Manager.

But how did the situation get to this point? Not only is the response from the assistant rude, but it lacks any ownership. My belief about this assistant is that they are mimicking the behaviour of the leaders around them in the belief that this customer service is acceptable. There could be unhealthy competition between the section managers where they are unwilling to help each other, including the customer, when they are from a different patch.

This can be driven by a lack of shop assistants, but the underlying culture is clearly lacking and is not being addressed. The actions and behaviours behind the scenes will quickly find their way to the shop floor and this example should be a red flag for the regional director and not just the store manager.

By now, you should be questioning how your customers see your team and what level of service they receive during each interaction. Don't fall into the trap of looking at customers from the perspective of people paying for your products and services. There are more customers than that in a business and you need to look widely at internal and external customers. If you do something for someone, they are your customer. Look at the following examples of poor customer service and see if you recognise any of the failings in your own team or business:

> *I don't like to complain on Twitter but absolutely shocking customer service from @vodafoneUK I've had no wi-fi since 4pm yesterday. First they denied there was a problem, then they said it was the green box. They keep saying it will be fixed ASAP - over 24 hrs on & zero service*
>
> *@PapaJohnsUK I used to love your pizza's, but haven't ordered from you in almost a year due to a really poor experience. Thought I'd give you another chance tonight.*
> *Food was cold, dry and tasteless, so it's been put in the right place. [Photo of a bin]*
>
> *@virginmedia after a very frustrating evening trying to get through to your service as my wifi will not connect and a possibly the worst website ever to access, can you resolve the issues in E15!!!*
>
> *@UberEats Canada there appears to be a technical issue with your technology - placed order 45 minutes ago and it got cancelled and I had to order again - called restaurant and they just received.*
>
> *Hey @GoPro! Ordered a HERO9 Black on 6/9, got a message it "shipped" 2-day air on 6/10, it's 6/17 but still no camera. Getting the run-around from customer service. HELP! #whereismygopro*
>
> *So disappointed with @FastSkips. Despite emailing & calling pleading with them to move the full skip, my requests have been ignored. They maybe fast at delivering & charging, but I've seen Turtle move faster at removing the skip*
>
> *Come on @AerLingus get someone on your phones. People need to know how they're getting home #stranded #stobartaircollapse*
>
> *Wow @Airbnb_uk, cancelled on a one nighter yesterday, then a host cancels on me and my young family on a 12 nighter with one hours notice and.....nothing from you. Even hung up on....shocking #customerexperience #retweet #airbnb*

The outcomes of bad customer service can be felt for many years and may need a re-brand to escape from the negativity that surrounds the business. Think about News International that changed their name to News UK[68] following the phone-hacking scandal. Although it was part of a wider re-organisation of the Murdoch-owned business, the effect was a distancing from the scandal of the past.

Other businesses have also changed their names, but these are not due to scandal, just the marketing machine finding a better way of pushing the new brand and image. What are the new names for these businesses?

Figure 7.1 – Previous names of businesses

Original Name	New Name
Peter's Super Submarines	
Backrub	
Jerry and David's Guide To The World Wide Web	
Blue Ribbon Sports	
Brad's Drink	
Relentless	
BT Cellnet	
Midland Bank	
Royal Mail	
Tokyo Tsushin Kogyo	
AuctionWeb	

The answers are in the activities section at the end of the chapter.

The renaming of a business or a brand due to a customer service failure, leadership scandal or quality failure is the pinnacle of how bad it can get. In many of the examples of poor customer service I have provided, the common ground is a lack of clear communication with customers. Every year we will see news reports from airports, train stations and ferry terminals of people who just want to know what is going on and why there is a delay. Businesses are often measured by the lowest level of leadership that is available in these circumstances as poor leaders will shrink into their shells and not want to communicate with their customers. This approach will simply store up the emotion and frustration until they find a way to express themselves.

Now it is time to explore some examples of great customer service. When you read these, you should be assessing the behaviours involved and also if you also have this present in your organisation:

> *Special shout out to @gmmerritt and the team at @DENAirport for helping this traveller make it to their flight today. There is a reason why you're North America's #1 Airport! #service*

#aboveandbeyond

Giving a shout out to @Walmart for excellent customer support via online chat with Kim. I needed to return an item that I purchased on Walmart Marketplace and was given a refund by Kim with very little back and forth. #customerloyalty #savemoney #livebetter

TY @PetSmart Just called your toll free Cust Svc for help with Treats program concern & your team member Savanah provided stellar support & service!!! #highfive #keepitup

@curryspcworld amazing service at #currysnorthwich tonight. Bought a washing machine, clicked and collected within 40 mins. I didn't even have to get out of the car.

@footlocker awesome service from Malli & Simeon at St David's, Cardiff Store Smiling face with sunglasses #Trainers #Sold

@LNER please thank your customer service staff in Leeds Bradford! They were so helpful and supportive when I missed my train and couldn't get home!! #northernhospitality #feelingthelove

To Liam at the @CostaCoffee stand at #DoncasterTrainStation this morning...YOU ROCK!!! I asked for the Champion Blend and he said "Of course... and not only that... I'm going to play you Champion by Chris Brown on my phone while I make it." AND he sang it too

@TheAA_UK fantastic service from Mickey this evening in West Wales, getting my car started, helpful, cheerful... definitely the best person if your car suddenly won't start! #helpful #thankyou

@SouthwestAir when things go awry (delay that will cause a missed connection) your people go out of their way to make it right. Muriel at the ticket counter at BDL was a star. won't fly any other airline.

@BarclaysUK great service Barclays, i lost my debit card Thursday night after 11:30pm reported it lost on the App and received a new one this morning before 9am - thank you #barclays #barclaysbank

@Tesco, Hi. I'd like to give a shout out to Mary in your Call centre. I received great service from Mary, she was so lovely & apologetic for an issue that was beyond your control. Please pass on my thanks; she's a credit to you! #tesco.

I would like to add my own to this list but not from Twitter. It was my first night at the Carlton in Singapore and I was trying to get connected to the internet for a crucial business call. Nothing was working. I could not get the Wi-Fi working on my business phone, personal phone or laptop. With time running out, I returned to reception to see that a flight had just arrived and all the reception agents were stacked with customers. I turned to the Concierge desk and asked for some help. One of the Concierge staff realised the urgency of the situation and rushed around the desk and ushered me to the lift. His colleague was already ringing their in-house IT team and passing on my room details. Within minutes, I was stood in my room watching two Concierge staff and an IT guy with a bunch of cables assessing every option with the internet. They discussed a few options and they stood back as they looked at the local news channel loading up on my laptop. Success! I completed my call and sent an email to the General Manager to thank him for the amazing service his team had provided. Within a few hours of sending the email, there was a knock at my door and I was presented with a box of chocolates and a hand-written card thanking me for recognising the efforts of the team. It should have been me buying the chocolates!

These examples of great customer service are delivered by people who are supported by sound leadership. A 'servant leader' (a leader who focuses primarily on the growth and well-being of people and the communities which they belong) will also strive to push aside barriers to allow great people to do a great job and I like to believe that is happening when customer driven leadership is in place. We do not need to see or hear from the leader to know that their influence is delivering an incredible experience for their customers. In the examples I have provided, there are people in crisis, some people just making a purchase and others dealing with an issue with the product or service. The way they are dealt with gives confidence, assurance and a feeling that they have been treated in a special way. These are some ingredients of customer service that all leaders can aspire to include in their business.

Global marketplace

Does customer driven leadership matter and is it worth the investment of time? I have seen people try to trade off customer service against short-term gains but then spend time dealing with complaints and escalations that have taken far greater resources to remedy. That is a simplistic look at a business case for customer driven leadership but the more important aspect that leaders should be considering is the impact of the globalization of markets.

The changing future of work sees greater automation, use of technology, a mobile workforce and globalisation of markets[69]. It is this globalization of markets that I wish to focus on. This is not just about the buying and selling of products, it also extends to the customer service that accompanies the purchases. You may consider yourself to be a small business with no impact in the global market, but you are wrong. You have an opportunity to access markets across the globe and stand out from the crowd by focusing on customer service.

There has been an increasing move to off-shoring of customer service centres and it is now a major industry for many countries. India, China, Malaysia, the Philippines, Brazil and Mexico are countries that have seen huge rises in the customer service industry. This burgeoning industry provides the opportunity for businesses to deliver 24/7 customer service across the globe. This now forms part of the value proposition for many businesses as they can focus on the delivery of products and services whilst still delivering an all-hours service.

Importantly, the emphasis on speed of communication to resolve issues is a key requirement for customers. We now live in an 'always-on' culture where customers expect to be able to browse, purchase and seek support for items throughout the day. The internet means that location is not a barrier and mobile phones with cheap calls mean that there is nothing stopping people from contacting a business to help with a problem. Selling products and services across the globe is now easier but your customer service needs to match the markets you target. If you have a mismatch, you will not be successful in the global marketplace.

There is a now legendary Twitter exchange that took place in 2013 between Hasan Syed and British Airways, after they lost his father's bag between Chicago and Paris.

> *@HVSN Sorry for the delay in responding, our twitter feed is open 0900-1700 GMT. Please DM your baggage ref and we'll look into this.*
>
> *@British_Airways how does a billion dollar corp only have 9-5 social media support for a business that operates 24/7? DM me yourselves.*

What makes this more incredible is that Hasan chose to promote the Tweet so by the time British Airways responded 8 hours later, it had been viewed over 76,000 times. This took place in 2013 which led the BBC's aviation consultant[70] to advise that "Airlines are going to have to start having 24/7 customer services and maybe they need to train up call centre reps to respond to messages on Facebook and Twitter." This may seem outdated but many years after this incident, some businesses are still coming to terms with providing customer service on a global basis.

Another notable example of unacceptable customer service can be found in Blake Morgan's book, Customer of the Future [71]. Blake discusses the example from Amazon where Jeff Bezos was discussing with his VP of Customer Service how long customers must wait on hold with the call centre. Bezos was assured that the maximum wait was a minute and then proceeded to call Amazon's customer service number. It took four and half minutes for Bezos to get through. The VP of Customer Service resigned shortly after this incident.

Seeing your processes and customer service through the eyes of the customer can be a key learning moment for a leader. Just as Bezos did, take a few minutes to experience your own level of service and decide if it is what you expected it to be. There have been many examples of the 'undercover boss' which sees a leader employed in the frontline of their business for a week. Their identity is masked and only at the end of the week do their colleagues discover who they really are. This is an extreme way of getting quick feedback on the level of customer service that is provided and often, quicker tests can be provided such as demonstrated by Bezos.

How can we provide a better customer service?

It was a privilege to welcome Blake Morgan onto my podcast where we had some fantastic discussions around her book and her thoughts about what is needed to provide customer driven leadership. Here is a short extract where Blake discusses the future of customer service, and she also includes a great story for you to consider.

> *We're still aiming for this one view of the customer where the customer doesn't have to work so hard to repeat themselves, when they call the bank and reach the credit card department. And now you must go to the checking card department. And these are basic things we've been trying to do for years.*
>
> *So I think the problem is that companies don't view the contact centre as an investment, they don't see it as a relationship building tool, they see it as a cost centre, they're still approaching it with a butts in seats mentality, they're still approaching it with how much what's the cost per call? What is the average handle time in the call centre, I think the goal is to be like Amazon to eliminate the need for the call centre and focus so much on cell service that the customer never needs to contact you.*
>
> *And that's really the trick. And then you can shift your very valuable people resources toward adding value to that customer rather than simply putting out fires. And there's a great example of this. And I'd actually like to take your listeners and viewers on a little break, please do this podcast and take you on a little walk next to a river. And let's imagine that you're walking on the banks of a river and you're with your best friend. Let's imagine*

each of you have your own best friend and your own River. So you're walking along the banks of a river and all of a sudden you hear somebody screaming and splashing and flailing your arms in the river. And you and your best friend realise that someone is drowning.

And so you and your best friend, dive into the river, swim over to that drowning person. And you guys together, drag her out of the water to safety. But as soon as you get to shore, you hear another person drowning in the river, and you and your friend swim over to the guy, you arduously drag him out.

But then when you get to shore, there's a third person drowning. And so again, you jump into the river, go to this drowning person, but you look up and you realise your friend has abandoned you. And you see him walking along the shore upstream. You say, hey, friend, where are you going? We have to save this drowning person. And he says to you, I'm going and walking upstream to figure out who's throwing all these people into the river. And the point of this parable for customer service is that we have this hero mentality where we love to be the hero. We love to save the day, but this is problem, because if we simply figured out why our customers are drowning, we wouldn't have to be the hero in the first place. And that should be the goal.

Blake's message is clear. You need to get ahead of saving your customers and start focusing on preventing the issues before they arise. Dealing with customer complaints and issues is time consuming and costly. More importantly, your customers will suffer and will not give recommendations to other potential customers. If you rely on repeat business from the same people, one poor customer experience could spell the end of your relationship with them.

Some businesses will seek to gain feedback from every interaction they have with their customers. These micro-surveys will be pop-ups on a computer screen or a simple voting system at the end of a call. If you are struggling to think if you have seen this, think about Microsoft Teams. At the end of most calls, I get a pop-up asking me to rate the quality of the call on a 5-star basis. You may have seen this same micro-survey on Microsoft Teams or another app. I like to believe that they are interested in the quality of the call, but I am sure they just want to hear that everything was 5-star!

Many businesses have invested heavily in this approach and have linked it to a Net Promoter Score[72] (NPS). Again, this will be happening around you even if you have not realised that your feedback may determine the bonus or continued employment of the person serving you. The NPS relies on a scale of 1-10 where businesses are hoping for a score of 9 or

10. The scoring is then assessed as follows:

Score	Classification
1-6	Detractor
7-8	Passive
9-10	Promotor

NPS Score = %Promotors minus %Detractors

On this system, businesses can be scored from -100 to 100. NICE Satmetrix provides a series of benchmarks and research around NPS so you can benchmark your business against your sector average. Department stores lead the way at 58, hotels at 39, banking at 35, mobile phone providers at 30 and satellite TV providers at 7. It is worthwhile reviewing their website and resources to see where your industry sits, especially if you use NPS.

I explained NPS to my family after a trip to buy a car had not gone to plan. We booked a test drive and my wife met the sales executive at the allotted time. After the drive, I could sense that my wife was not impressed with the sales executive who had failed to build any rapport and she had an attitude that could not be overlooked. When the sales executive disappeared to 'consult with the manager' we were discussing the perspex screen that separated us from the cash register. Pinned to the perspex screen was a poorly photocopied survey form with lots of yellow and orange highlights on the boxes for 9 and 10. Written on the top of the page was "* Please rate your experience as 10 *" and at the foot of the page "* You will receive this survey 24 hours after your visit. It is important to us*".

Once I had explained the purpose of the survey and the reason for the plea for a rating of 9 or 10, the poor customer service we received became funny. We did not buy a car that day but went home looking forward to receiving our NPS survey. Unfortunately, it never arrived as we were both really wanted to provide feedback on our experience.

What metrics do you have in place to monitor your customer service? If you do have measures in place, when was the last time you stopped to see if they were still measuring the right aspect of your business? Many businesses have moved on over the last few years and have been driven by changes in their external environment yet they have retained old customer service measures which were designed for a previous way of working. To provide a better customer service, you need to be aware of where in the chain you need to improve to stop 'saving' people. Some businesses will have NPS scores for different parts of their process chain to understand where the improvement is necessary. Unless you have some understanding of which part to improve, you will not get to the root cause of the issues.

Five pillars of customer driven leadership

I have given many examples of how customer service can fail, and the impact it has on customers, and the great examples where businesses have delivered customer service that was more than the customer expected. There are some commonalities amongst these examples and along with my own research into this area, I have identified five pillars of customer driven leadership (Figure 7.2).

- Role modelling – Unless you have leaders, throughout your business that are acting as a role model for others to follow, you will never succeed in developing a culture of customer driven leadership. Role modelling is not an initiative that you can grow from the ground up and hope that it catches on. Leaders need to provide the direction and example. They need to hold each other to account and in turn, other people will hold to account people in their own departments and elsewhere. If you're not prepared to do this, there is no point in trying any other pillar.

- Empowerment – Building in complex escalation routes for your people to jump through to deliver customer service is not going to work. Empowering your people to act, without endorsement from someone else, is liberating for your employees and your customers. This requires great leadership to create the environment of trust on both sides, employer and employee, and clear communication about the level of empowerment given to employees.

- Clarity – This leads on from empowerment. Unless you can clearly articulate the boundaries for your people, there will not be true empowerment. Indeed, you could create confusion and slow down a process that is designed to speed up the delivery of customer service. The test to ensure you have this correct is to ask your employees what delegated authority they have been given to resolve customer issues quickly and effectively. If they struggle to answer, you have not delivered the clarity they needed. If they give the wrong answer, you have not given the clarity they needed.

- Exceeding expectations – Customer driven leadership is not just about providing the minimum you can get away with. That level of customer service is available within most products and services. Your competitors are providing that now as their standard and aiming to go above it. You need to aim far beyond the basic provision and deliver customer service that is talked about in the press, aspired to by other professionals and sought after by customers. You can only do this by exceeding the expectations of your customers during every interaction and this must be 'in the moment'. Once that moment to shine has passed, you have lost the opportunity.

Figure 7.2 – Five pillars of customer driven leadership

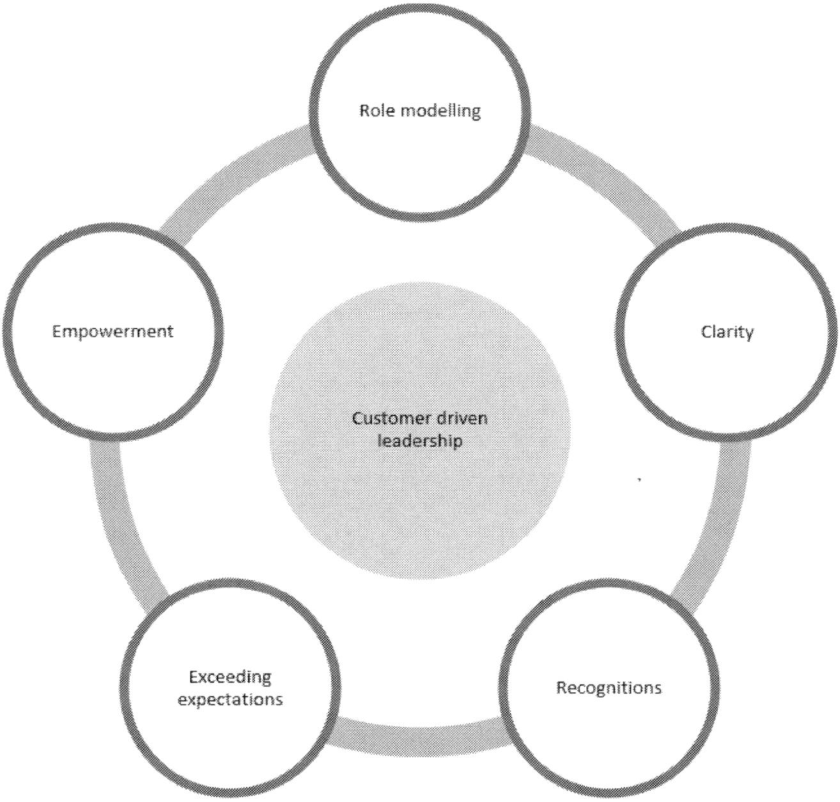

- Recognition – What do you do when your employees deliver fantastic customer service? You should not hesitate to recognise the contribution of your people when they deliver the customer service that you are striving to deliver. This requires thought about how you are going to do this at scale, not just for the odd example. Whilst you're considering the issue of scale, now think about the appropriateness of the recognition. Set your route to recognition too high, and it will be a costly venture. Set your recognition too low and it will be costly in that people seldom deliver the customer service you strive for. More important than the level of recognition is the timing. It must be immediate. If you have developed a system of nominations, committees and awards panels, you have lost.

You can use these five pillars to assess your own preparedness for customer driven leadership. Here are some questions to ask within your business to understand what gaps you have in these areas.

Figure 7.3 – Discovery questions for the five pillars

Pillar	Question
Role modelling	Are your leaders accessible to employees and customers?
	Do your leaders actively role model behaviours required within the business?
	Are your people able to challenge leaders about how they are seen by employees and customers?
	Do you have a staff survey or 360 degree reporting process that allows for feedback to leaders?
	Are your leaders held to account when they fall short of the role model they are meant to be?
Empowerment	Do your employees feel trusted?
	Do you actively empower your employees to take decisions and resolve issues without the need for escalation?
	Is empowerment instilled across the business or in small pockets?
	Do your leaders drive empowerment and push back when employees escalate issues that they can resolve?
Clarity	How do you communicate the level of empowerment to your employees?
	Is empowerment discussed and made clear through the onboarding process and within induction training?
	Do you constantly reinforce the drive for customer service and why it matters?
	Is customer service openly discussed at team meetings?
	Do you re-clarify the boundaries of empowerment when things go wrong?
Exceeding expectations	Do your employees know the basic level of customer service that is expected?
	Do you openly discuss the need for exceeding customer expectations?
	Do you know your champions of customer service who regularly exceed customer expectations?

Pillar	Question
	How do you spread good practice between teams?
Recognition	Do you celebrate when your employees deliver great customer service?
	Do you pass on feedback direct to employees from customers?
	How do you curate the stories of customer service so they form part of your culture?
	Are stories of customer service included in your induction?
	How do you reward employees for continually delivering great customer service?

Where you have struggled to answer the question or you are not doing the activity to the level you want, this is an indication of an area to explore. This assessment can be made more powerful by inviting several people to contribute from different departments.

Challenge each other's assumptions and be honest with your answer to get the most out of the exercise. There is nothing wrong with having gaps and putting a plan in place to address the gap!

Summary

With competition for services and products increasing every day, the biggest standout will always be customer experience. Winning the battle for customers is only possible if the business has customer driven leadership at its heart and not a superficial statement on a wall. Role modelling, clarity, exceeding expectations, empowerment and recognition are the factors needed to build customer driven leadership. Then, your technology processes also need to be aligned to help identify hot spots and cold spots within the business so action can be taken to address issues quickly. This includes the ability to react to social media posts and see this as an opportunity to create an impression with your customer base.

Reflective activities

- What is the best customer service you have ever received? What was it about that experience that made it so good?

- Who in your business is the epitome of customer service? What makes them stand out?

- Do you see customer service as a cost or an advantage?

- Is customer service a department or is it everyone responsible?

- Review if your customer service measures are still fit for your business.

Activities

Answers to the businesses who have changed their name.

Original Brand	New Brand
Peter's Super Submarines	Subway
Backrub	Google
Jerry and David's Guide To The World Wide Web	Yahoo!
Blue Ribbon Sports	Nike
Brad's Drink	Pepsi
Relentless	Amazon
BT Cellnet	O2
Midland Bank	HSBC
Royal Mail	Consignia (now back to Royal Mail!)
Tokyo Tsushin Kogyo	Sony
AuctionWeb	EBay

Suggested reading

- Morgan B. (2019). *Customer of the Future: 10 Guiding Principles for Winning Tomorrow's Business*. Harper Collins: USA.

- Schaefer M. (2019). *Marketing Rebellion: The Most Human Company Wins.*

Chapter 8

High performing teams

"Great things in business are never done by one person. They're done by a team of people."
Steve Jobs (Former CEO of Apple)

Introduction

When you think of high performing teams, what comes to mind? For many people, they jump straight to a sports team as the outcome is easy to measure.

Mark England[73], Team GB's Chef de Mission, said of the 2021 British Olympic team: "For this team to deliver 65 medals is absolutely extraordinary," and "History on the back of the most complex, challenging and difficult environment that we will ever face, certainly in my lifetime." The outcome at the Tokyo Olympics exceeded the expectations of the British Olympic Association and he believed that "Against all odds, it is the greatest achievement in British Olympic history" he continued "It has been the miracle of Tokyo".

Have you stopped to consider how Leicester City Football Club won the Premier League in 2015-2016 when they started as 5000-1 outsiders? They won the league by 10 points, had a win rate of 60% and spent a total of £26 million during the transfer window. (In the same transfer window Manchester City spent £49 million on just one player, Raheen Sterling.) Their players excelled as Jamie Vardy set a record for scoring in consecutive games and Riyad Mahrez was voted the Player's Player of the Year.

Bringing the focus on high performance teams back to business, Henry Ford and his team of engineers set out to deliver his vision that automobile transport could be made affordable through mass production. They focused on efficiency and eventually creating the assembly line. Part of this plan included attracting and retaining the best workers by increasing their pay and reducing the number of working hours. Together they changed the way the world travelled.

A final example is Walt Disney's creation of a studio that made household names out of cartoon characters. Not only this, but they were also incredibly profitable. Disney worked closely with Ub Iwerks (the creator of Mickey Mouse) to build a team of '9 old men' who were the animators behind the scenes. In 2020, Walt Disney Company[74] had assets of $200 billion and a global revenue of $65 billion.

This chapter will examine what constitutes a high performing team and how a leader can create and lead a high performing team to be successful like some of the teams I have already mentioned. This chapter will include examples of self-managing teams to understand how radical changes in hierarchy can contribute to higher performance.

What constitutes a high performing team?

Mihaly Csikszentmihalyi's[75] book Flow describes a state of flow which I see in high performing teams. As we redefine our future leaders to focus on a collaborative environment where people feel free to craft their job, we need flow to underpin it. As a leader, you should understand that flow affects your business on a daily basis and contributes to your bottom line. Csikszentmihalyi noted that "*Workers who are in control of how to do their job are likely to spend more of their time at work in flow, be more engaged in what they do, and work at their peak capacity*."

When employees are at their happiest and most engaged at work, they are in the flow. This then makes them highly productive. And the opposite is equally true. So, when people are disgruntled and disengaged, employees are not as productive and could even lead to a toxic atmosphere. At some point, we have all been in the flow. When working with customers, I find myself in the flow. Hours pass by in a flash. I am positively challenged and my skills are adequate. According to Csikszentmihalyi, I am in state of ecstasy where nothing else matters and this is me at my most productive. And it is where we need our people to be within a high-performing team.

In applying this to your own organisation, how useful would it be to understand which employees were in the flow? Or more importantly, which ones were out of the flow and were not as productive as they could be? I know that many people reading this will claim they already know who is in or out of the flow. But what about those steady and silent people who just keep their head down and keep working. Are they truly in the flow or just getting by?

Another primary component of finding flow is timely feedback. Csikszentmihalyi noted that "Immediate feedback allows the individual to make slight alterations to behaviour that guides progress." This should be a primary feature for leaders looking to support high performing teams. Knowing that people are in or out of flow simply is not enough. There needs to be a feedback loop to their manager to highlight that an employee is out of the flow and that they should hold a check-in to discuss this with the employee. We need to move our people to a place where they once again feel ecstasy and where nothing else matters.

This is easy to see in a performance bell curve where we will see that an average business has employees with a range of abilities. The left-hand side sees lower abilities (few people), the middle performing people represent the bulk of the business and the right-hand side sees the highest performers (few people).

Figure 8.1 – High performers in a business

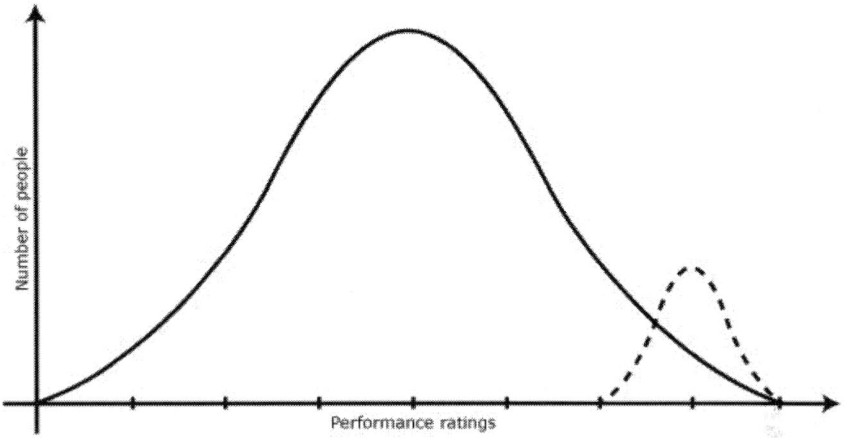

If we then identified a high performing team on the same graph, the predominance of the people is in the higher end of the performance range. The number of high performers is because even the 'weaker' people within a high performing team are higher performers than most of the people in the business. This team will have a disproportionate number of high performers compared to the rest of the business.

McKinsey[76] believe that "What often separates the highest-performing organizations from the rest is culture." This focus on culture as a foundation of high performing teams correctly places the culture of the team as a foundational ingredient to the team's success. In a perfect world, this should be the business culture and not just the team culture.

However, it is often the influence, presence and motivational competences of the team leader that makes this more localised. Business have tried many times over to replicate a high performing culture into other part of the business but this too often fails as the leader with the drive to make it happen is not transferred to the new team.

Constituents of a high performing team

A high performing team may not be the most obvious to identify within a business. There is no one identifiable activity that would indicate high performance and many people who tell you they work in a high performing team may be hyping up their team.

I have experienced the pleasure of working in teams that were regarded as high performing by other parts of the business. This gives confidence to the people in the team and spreads confidence throughout the rest of the business. Their services are sought widely as they are regarded as reliable people who will deliver on any project they are involved with. Often regarded as the 'trump card' when creating new teams, their pedigree of coming from a high performing team established trust and confidence in others.

I see high performing teams sharing many of the same attributes. Combined with research from McKinsey, Forbes[77] and some excellent books including Gilbert's *Human Competence*[78], here are my constituents of a high performing team:

Figure 8.2 – Constituents of a high performing team

	Information	Instrumentation	Motivation
Environment	**Feedback** This requires constant communication and feedback between a leader and their team. This includes 121 feedback on how to improve performance and transparency about the business objectives.	**Culture** The culture of the business will affect the ability of the business to create and maintain high performing teams. Develop an environment where people support colleagues and feel able to challenge decisions.	**Incentives** This is both intrinsic and extrinsic. High performance demands suitable financial reward but people also need to feel they have grown as a team. Show appreciation and recognise the contribution of the team.
Behaviour	**Knowledge** Leaders need to develop their people and ensure they stay ahead of any learning requirement. Provide appropriate development to support high performance and enable professionals to grow their knowledge.	**Capacity** Ensure that the needs of the business are maintained and that clear lines of succession are in place for others to join a high-performance team. The transparency over what competences roles require are key.	**Motives** Does the employee achieve a state of flow in their role? Are they suited to the role or could they be better elsewhere? Is the employee committed to shared ownership and the principal that everyone shares in the successes and failures?

The model provided by Glbert gives direction that the 'environment' issues should be addressed first as these are the easiest ones to tackle. The 'behaviours' are more difficult as they are based on the actions of individuals and require more effort to resolve. You may wish to amend these attributes further to fit with your environment and the language you use. I advise that you consider how you are going to measure these attributes or support a transparent system. You may already have the technology to do this, you may be able to tweak your existing technology stack to achieve the outcome or you may be willing to purchase a piece of software.

However, high performance does not arrive at the doorstep of a leader or a team. It takes time and energy to build, and then more time and energy to maintain. The focal point for this effort is the leader setting the vision and creating the environment for a high performing team to flourish. But that requires a leader to be able to lead confidently so they are seen as a role model. Many leaders have bouts of imposter syndrome. (Please note I mention 'bouts' instead of just one episode.) Imposter Syndrome 'refers to an internal experience of believing that you are not as competent as others perceive you to be'[79]. It makes people feel like they are fake and have just been incredibly lucky to be where they are today. This feeling is not just reserved for business leaders and we can see this in many public personalities.

Dr Ben Ritter is a coach and wellbeing consultant with a particular interest for Imposter Syndrome. We discussed imposter syndrome on my podcast and here are Ben's thoughts about this experience and some strategies to deal with it:

> *"Where do you feel like you're an imposter? And some people say, well, it's something that you haven't done very often. Some people that are in the spotlight -celebrities, famous actors, huge leadership experts and gurus - will tell you, "I've got the voices there, it talks to me, you're not good enough". And if you look at people that are high achievers, and strive for a lot, and maybe even have achieved a lot, they, may be motivated by this "you're not good enough" voice, which is really dangerous.*
>
> *Because if you don't achieve certain things that can really become impactful on your mental health and lead to some serious issues. As people talk me through the moments that you feel like an imposter, and usually that happens when someone is going to want to like to create a podcast or they enter a networking event, when people can meet each other in person, they think everyone's judging them or everyone's really making fun of them in a way.*
>
> *So they're stuck in their own head, whenever someone was feeling like they're an imposter.*
> *It's because they're listening to the voices in their head that are telling them that they're an imposter. And those usually tend to stay there for a while, especially when it deals with things that are important to you, the more important you tend to feel something is, the more likely you're going to have voices that*

create doubt the and activate the fear that's within you the discomfort that's within you. And so, when you're looking to deal with imposter syndrome, it's understanding first where you feel like an imposter and actually listening to the voices. Very often, we tend to push them away, we tend to avoid the fear, we tend to avoid the discomfort and we don't actually try to understand why I feel like an imposter.

Where in my life do I feel like an imposter? And at the same time, why not throw some positivity in the mix and say, "Where do I feel like I'm a champion?" Why do I feel like I'm just crushing it in life? And take a look at both situations and ask yourself, "How did I get to this point?" And just for a general level of awareness? Because the next step is what you have to actually change the programmes, you have to change the voices in your head, because right now you're listening to this person with the microphone says you're not good enough.

And so, what you have to do is you have to initially take away the microphone, and you have to start screaming back at it, while you're good enough, the reasons why you're good enough. Because no matter what you do, if you just try to push past these voices, they're going to be there unless you reprogram and reframe them and start believing other voices more that you're never going to actually get over it.

So, you literally have to write down your belief that is holding you back where you feel like an imposter. Rewrite it in a way that is more positive and self-serving that you believe that is supported with evidence that you found from the introspection from the activity of understanding where you're crushing it in life. And then tell yourself that three to four times a day it's something we have to do to start creating new programmes in our mind that serve us that support us and champion in us.

Because that doubt, that imposter, is going to be there. Because they're going to be moments in your life where you have you failed miserably, where you are feeling down or you're feeling sad, you're feeling depressed. Just because emotions are a roller coaster, we can't control them, we just choose how we react to them. And so, we have to get used to actually creating this voice in our head, that's a greater champion that's louder. And to do that, we do literally need to sit there and practice it each and every single day."

A leader should make time to focus on themselves, because until they are confident and ready to lead a high performing team, they need to develop their confidence. If you have read Ben's excellent advice on imposter syndrome and recognised any of the symptoms, you may need to take time to find a coach to help you through this phase. Making time for yourself is fundamental to leading a high performing team.

How can a leader create a high performing team?

Creating a high performing team does not happen overnight. It often requires a major shift within a team; e,g. turnover of people, relocation or new project, to present an uncomfortable situation which people are energised to make better. Taking our attributes which were based on Gilbert's work, we can break these down into the requirements for a high performing team.

- **Feedback** – Timely and clear feedback are the basic requirements here. Leaders need to make individual feedback their reason for being at work to enable their people to grow. Communication with the team, including feedback on team goals, is critical to build a transparent culture where people can support each other to achieve greater goals. Self-reflection is important following feedback sessions so people can assess what they can do differently to achieve stretch targets. The feedback and communication should be readily available in a HR system where people can review their progress and provide direct comment to their management team. Business communications should be clear and available to everyone with the option to ask follow-up questions that are answered promptly. Feedback is a two-way flow of information and leaders should be prepared to listen to the feedback from their team to understand how they can better support the team in the future. This can be during a check-in or through a discussion group for 'Ask the CEO'. Check-ins support this approach as they provide the opportunity for leaders and their team to have open discussions. Both parties can start a check-in and there is no set timeframe. As they are not determined by the organisation, there is a shared power between the leader and employee and both have an interest in the outcomes of the check-in.

- **Culture** – The culture is central to a high performing team. This needs to be set and role modelled by the leaders. The publication of a shared vision and business values enable a high performing team to have a ground zero that they can always return to for clarity. Over time, the vision may need to change to reflect the changing circumstances but this needs to be communicated throughout the team and remain accessible to everyone. When leaders see people acting against the business values, not subscribing to the business vision or acting in a way that destabilises the culture, they must act quickly. The leader must support and challenge people to constantly provide a point of reference.

- **Incentives** – Leaders must ensure that people are rewarded fairly for their contribution and their reward strategy is clear. Confusion about salary, commissions, awards etc causes people to lose focus on the delivery of their outputs. Any changes to an agreed reward strategy must be communicated quickly and with clarity to reduce the amount of disruption that will be caused for people. The more intrinsic incentives are just as important. A recognition scheme, embedded in a HR system, gives a space where people can publicly thank their peers for their contribution and provides a way of acknowledging their assistance. The difference between this and other schemes is that it is 'in the moment'. There is no requirement for a manager to authorise the recognition and it does not require a committee to agree to the award of a recognition. It is recorded on the HR system and can be reviewed by colleagues to see the recognitions they have received. These can also be linked to business values to identify how they have shown the values that the business has identified as key to its success.

- **Knowledge** – Continual learning is a requirement for high performing teams. This approach to learning is required at all levels of the team and is an indicator of how people are adjusting to changes in the environment. People gain knowledge from many different sources including informal learning, on the job training and formal training courses. Businesses need to provide access to a range of learning resources so people can learn at their own pace, to suit their own style and accessed through a medium of their choice. Businesses cannot simply provide one option as this does not help people to grow with the demands of a rapidly changing environment. Learning Management Systems which are integrated to the HR system are now the norm for businesses who believe in the active development of high performing teams. Both leaders and their people should be able to access their learning record which can then be discussed at a check-in. Further learning through secondments or shadowing should also be identified to help provide a wider range of business understanding. These are powerful conversations to have in a check-in which help the leader underline their commitment to the development of their people.

- **Capacity** – Leaders need to continually plan for turnover within a high performing team. Some turnover provides a benefit as it enables new people with fresh ideas to enter the team and challenge current assumptions. Succession is required to support a healthy turnover rate and this can come from within the business or from outside. Internal succession can be enhanced if the HR system has a way of identifying the required competences/qualifications and then performing a search for suitable candidates. These people may be quicker to move into the high performing team and require less time to become effective when compared with external candidates. Additionally, if the succession planning is done openly and with prior discussion, the identified successors can be trained and developed so they are ready to move into any future vacancy. External talent pools should offer the same identification of potential candidates against a set of clearly required competences and qualifications. The external candidates should also be kept informed about developments and opportunities within the business. If done correctly, this provides another ready pool of people who can move into the high performing team when a vacancy arises.

- **Motives** – A recruitment process that reliably identifies people who are motivated to achieve the same results underpins the establishment of a high performing team. The time taken to identify talent and then select the right candidate will deliver long term rewards for a high performing team. Recruitment of new people into an established team is always a risk but this needs to be minimised. Including a 'meet the team' session as part of the selection process will allow team members to give their own evaluation of the candidates including if their motivations are aligned to the rest of the team. This needs to continue during the onboarding process to ensure a smooth transition into the team. For existing team members, check-ins again give the opportunity for leaders to continually assess if people are still motivated correctly and focussed on delivering the correct outcomes. People who are regarded as a flight risk can be identified and then the risk can be mitigated by the leader. The recruitment, onboarding and flight risk assessment should also be contained within the HR system. These are not separate activities that are dealt with by a different department and the leader must be central to these activities. Flow is also an indicator of an individual's motivation for work. If they can never achieve a state of flow, this should immediately indicate a risk that a leader should act upon with an honest conversation.

These items can be supported by a quality HR system which provides insights to leaders and gives a basis for good communication across the team. This should be no surprise given my background in HR technology! It is important not to be over reliant on the technology as it will not do a leader's job for them. Given the right HR system, it will inform a leader, provide valuable insights, enable them to automate a lot of their repetitive work and prompt discussions given certain triggers within this system. However, it will not replace an open conversation which is led with empathy.

How can a leader support a team to give them the freedom to deliver above the average team?

The six requirements I have outlined for a high performing team are not delivered by magic. A leader must be able to look after a team and create the environment for them to succeed. The discussion on Servant Leadership in Chapter 3 described how leaders can support their teams and remain in the background. There are many actions and behaviours a leader can display which helps a team to reach a level of high performance. Here are 8 actions and behaviours that are needed for a leader to deliver the requirements I have outlined:

Figure 8.3 – 8 actions and behaviours for leaders

Many of these actions require practice! They are often seen as the softer side of leadership but, they deliver the hardest outcomes. As a new leader, you may need to spend time with your mentor or coach working through what these actions mean for you and how to improve. Never be afraid to ask leaders how they achieve some of these actions or what were the circumstances when they failed to deliver on these actions.

Always be on the look out for capability gaps in your team. You should be constantly assessing your team to spot looming gaps and then take preventative action which avoids a dip in your high performing team. Your role is to then push through the levels of bureacracy to deliver resources or remove barriers which are preventing your team from progressing. Clearing the way for your team is an ongoing task and is something you should be in the habit of looking at on a regular basis. If you think that everyone has the resources they need and the barriers have been removed, you have missed something! Look again, speak to people and find out what is needed.

In the next section I am going to look at some examples where teams have failed to deliver and some leadership failings that contributed to these failures. This may also help you to understand why these are important and to learn from the failures of other leaders.

How diversity supports high performing teams

As a teenager, when I got frustrated with people or situations, my mum told me "Wouldn't the world be boring if everyone was like you!". It took me many years to get to understand what she meant and even now I can hear those words when I am frustrated with a lack of progress on a project or when people have acted in a way that was unnecessary. This has stuck with me and helped me question the appropriateness of teams and identify where a lack of diversity is working against teams who are trying to achieve high performance.

It is clear to me that high performance rests on the diversity of people within the team. Because of this I take my hat off to people who have started to publicly 'out' organisations and panels which have no diversity. Andy Street[80], West Midlands Mayor, refused to serve on a panel for "2022: A year of celebration" which had an all-male panel at the Conservative Party Conference in October 2021. He has a policy of refusing to serve on panels where no women are included. This lack of diversity is now an issue which has been named 'manels[81]' - panels consisting of males. Other public figures and leaders have announced they will not take part in manels and this is now being openly discussed.

This does not mean that we should resort to tokenism of any kind but create an environment where diversity is really valued for the wide experiences that are brought to the team. This need for diversity is not just about gender split or ethnicity but on professional background. What has always fascinated me about work is hearing about the background of people and the journey they have taken to be where they are.

I have worked with a HR Director who started her career in nursing, a Finance Director that had trained as a plumber and an Electrician that had worked as a Geography teacher for 20 years. Each one brought something from their previous profession to their current working life which made them more effective and interesting! For those colleagues who have interests outside of work such as volunteering, Scouting, Guiding, School Governor, small business owner etc they also bring a wealth of diversity.

During an interview, I always like to find out what people do outside of work and understand the extra leadership roles that people willingly undertake for no financial reward. The learning they get from this community experience is then brought back into the business and is a rich source of market data. I am not the only person who looks for these extra activities that provide a rich leadership experience. If you have an interest outside of work and you are being interviewed for a job, make sure to tell the interviewers about your other experiences! It could be the slight advantage you require!

Do you actively create a diverse environment? Your recruitment process is the starting point to this question but it is complemented by the leaders who seek to listen to the people who break the mould. People will still try to 'hire in their own shadow' and this can only be overcome by adopting a range of selection processes coupled with a diverse recruitment panel. You should be able to see the statistics for your hiring campaigns and see where your candidates dropped out of the process. If you really want to change the outcomes, and this should be a key aim for a leader, you need to consider who was on the recruitment panel. There has been a considerable amount written on removing bias from recruitment processes but, it is the people conducting the process that make the decision on who to hire.

As a leader you should take part in their processes and challenge areas that need to be improved. Challenge the interviewers about what questions they did not ask and why they felt the need to ask the questions they did ask. In some cases, you may want to re-interview people to see if they could be a fit for your business. If you do see practices that are stopping a diverse mix of people in the business, you must take action. You are the role model when assembling your team and you must hold your team to the same standards you set. A high performing team rests on the quality and diversity of the people within it - you must champion this approach.

Here is an extract from the podcast with Mark Schaefer who related a story of a CEO committing to altering the diversity within his business:

> *"I won't name the company, but I was working with a company, a big multinational company. They came out with this announcement. The CEO had this very formal setting and this script. By the way, this is a company where the entire executive board is white, and there's one female on the entire Executive Board of this global company. So, he said "Well in response to all this attention around doing the right thing and the activism. We're making a commitment today to double the number of African American employees in our company". Now, to me it's kind of tone deaf, because it seems like the right thing, but that's something they should have done in the 80s. You look at the board and you say, "that's the problem". You don't even have anybody on the board. And then even the term African American isn't really the term that's being used today, because there's a lot of people of colour that may not have an African heritage.*
>
> *That's a company still following the script. There's no empathy. There's no feeling. There's no understanding. You're reading something that a lawyer put in front of you. I'm not saying it's a*

bad thing. Maybe it's the best that culture can do right now. And it is an evolution. But I mean, to me a statement like that you're so far behind. Where are you and where you need to be. Where's the where's the vulnerability? Here's what I want to hear him say. "Wow, we have been so wrong. Look at our board. I look around wonder where have we been in this world? I'm personally committed, this is what I'm going to do. This is what I'm going to do as the leader of this company to move this company, not just check a box and fill a quota. But I want to change the company, the culture of that company. This is what I'm responsible for. I'm going to change the culture of this company to be more understanding, more inclusive, fairer to everyone". That's what I want to hear."

Mark has some great thoughts here especially around the personal commitment of the leader to make a change because they are rooted in the change that is needed. This commitment is how a leader should begin to make a meaningful change to create diversity within a business.

What are self-managing teams?

Now we have talked about the impact a leader can make on a team to deliver higher than normal performance and ow diversity is part of this, what about teams that shun the idea of a manager or leader? Did you know they exist? There are many examples where teams self-organise their work, decide on hiring and agree reward strategies. These teams are not limited to businesses with a few people but also larger enterprises. Here are some examples of teams driving high performance without appointed managers:

- Buurtzorg[82] - Jos De Blok established Buurtzorg, a Dutch healthcare business, in 2006 with a team of 4 nurses. This has now grown to over 14,000 nurses operating in self-managing teams of no more than 12 people. Although there are 50 Administrative staff and 18 coaches, there are no managers. Their 1000+ teams have received a lot of attention from researchers for their approach which has delivered one of the highest scores for employee satisfaction in Dutch businesses above 1000 people. Each team consists of people in seven roles: the main role, the housekeeper, the informer, the developer, the team player, the planner and the mentor. But there is no team leader.

- Zappos[83] - Since 2014, Zappos have adopted Holocracy and self-management. ZapposInsights[84] defines Holocracy as '...like an operating system for your organization. It is a predefined set of rules and processes, checks and balances, and guidelines that an organization can use to help them become self-managed and self-organized by giving every employee (instead of just management) the power to innovate, make changes, and have a voice.' Their aim of doing this is to enable each team to think and act like a small business to deliver quicker decision making and remove bottlenecks. In 2019, Zappos[85] had online sales of $537 million and achieved a growth rate of 6%.

- Haier[86] - With a global turnover of $39 billion in 2018, Haier are manufacturers of home appliances with offices in over 160 countries. Their 80,000 people have been split into 2,000 self-organising teams. The Chairman of Haier, Zhang Ruimin believes that "The bosses are not customers so why should the workers listen to them? They have changed their business so the focus is entirely on the user and not on the traditional command and control structures of the past. After acquiring Sanyo White Goods in 2011[87], they quickly removed the seniority-based compensation schemes and replaced them with rewards for people creating value.

What should stand out about these examples is that the leaders (Jos De Blok, Tony Hiersh and Zhang Ruimin) had a vision. Not only did they have a vision they could tell people about, but they trusted people to deliver their vision for them. Their role was to provide the environment for their teams to succeed and provide the platform for them to build their self-managing teams. What this does is to flatten the structures across the business which speeds up decision making and empowers people to act. Self-managing teams are not simply letting people do what they want to do. The teams will require a clear vision and set of goals for them to organise how they are going to achieve the outcomes. Mike Seavers[88], ex-CTO from Riot Games asks his team if they are clear on the vision and the goals. He encourages people to constantly think about the stated vision and goals to determine their way forward.

Summary

Leaders need to focus on shifting both mindsets and behaviours to achieve high performance within their teams. At the same time, leaders also need to change to move away from focusing on tactical issues to delivering strategic value. This includes removing barriers and providing resources so their teams can be successful – true servant leadership! For the final sporting analogy, the football manager is not on the pitch during the game. They must clarify their vision and goals before the game and then trust the team to perform. When creating the environment for people to thrive and grow into a high-performance team, trust sits at the centre of this environment. Without trust, team will never reach their potential of high performance.

Reflective activities

- Think about the most junior person on you team, are they trusted and empowered to act to deliver your vision and your goals?
- Look at my constituents of a high performing team, based on Gilbert's BEM model. Apply this to your business and plan to address any gaps you identify.
- Consider how you could use self-managing teams in your business. Can you provide the right leadership and environment for self-managing teams to flourish?

Suggested reading

- Freedman A. (2021). *Thrive*. Lioncrest Publishing.
- Gilbert T. (1996). *Human Competence*. HRD Press. Massachusetts.

Part 3

Leadership for the future

Chapter 9

Networks

"Skilled leaders tend to have resonance with a wide circle of people – and have a knack for finding common ground and building rapport. That doesn't mean they socialize continually; it means they work under the assumption that nothing important gets done alone. Such leaders have a network in place when the time for action comes."
Daniel Goleman[89] (Author)

Introduction

Networks are the life blood of a successful leader. In turn, networks support business success but they are not the sole reason for business success. For anyone about to turn to the next chapter, let me assure you that networking is not just about joining a golf club but this could be part of your network. There are a terrific number of opportunities now available online to supplement the existing face-to-face networking opportunities at conferences, professional bodies, charitable foundations or as part of a local sports team. The online opportunities are even greater and growing by the day. This includes the 'hangouts' which can occur on Twitter and other platforms where people will meet once a week for a discussion about a given topic.

Taking part in a webinar can lead to connections with people in your industry or even potential clients who you had no idea existed until they asked a question in a webinar. Or, as a podcast host, the amount of people you can get access to and build a network of global thought leaders and experts. There are many ways to build your network and, in this chapter, we will discuss how and why you can do this. This will include a focus on the use of social media and how this presence can help to build a network and access a wider network compared with the traditional sources. In this chapter I will focus on professional networks and outline why these remain important in a globalised environment.

Traditional vs non-traditional networks

Who had a roller-deck full of contacts? Or a box containing hundreds of business cards that occasionally you would rifle through looking for someone you met last year? This might seem like a strange concept for some leaders reading this but it's true! Regardless of how you came by those business cards, you had a network of people to contact. Networking businesses have grown to support gatherings where people can meet, discuss and receive a keynote speech from an event sponsor.

I've certainly taken part in many of these activities with varied success.

The non-traditional networks have now emerged. These include LinkedIn, Twitter, communities within each of these platforms and even newer spaces such as Clubhouse. One of the best run and engaged online community I have been part of is the #HRHour on Twitter. The coordinator hosts a weekly event, every Thursday, with 2 questions to start the discussions. There is some moderation/encouragement but otherwise, it's a great way to meet fellow professionals, discuss topical items and learn from each other. After the event, I also make a point of following the contributors to the discussion to grow my network. By using social media to help build my network, I can cross time zones and borders to connect with people I would not otherwise get to meet. This has been one of the biggest advantages of the non-traditional networking events.

You may have noticed that business have sprung up to support the growth of networks online. According to one website, I can buy 2500 followers on Twitter for $99 but there are many other offers where I can buy tens of thousands at a time. Building a following through this method is not for me and I don't suggest you do it either. Your real contacts will see straight through this and eventually, you will realise that this number means nothing and holds no value to you. The numbers of followers are only applicable for the vain. Real leaders don't worry about the numbers and concentrate solely on the quality.

The reality is there is no traditional and non-traditional network. There is now just a network. Some of your network may be in person and others may be virtual. For many of your network, this is a seamless experience as you interact with them across a platform and in-person. In this chapter I cover a lot of information which is aimed at the whole of your network, including the use of social media to build and maintain a network. It would be wrong to separate out social media into its own chapter as it is intertwined in the fabric of networks. This brings its own benefits and pitfalls as I will discuss.

Understanding networking from an early age

My father was a great role model for building a network of contacts throughout the country in a variety of industries and with people of all levels in business. This extended through to a more personal network of people who he had met through his Church and other social activities. He was always keen to meet new people and understand the connections they had in common. I would often see him introducing people who had never met before and when doing so, explaining the connection they had with each other or with him. He helped people to make networks and he did it without realising what he was doing.

He always knew the right person to speak to. This included speaking to his tailor and then acquiring the shirt material from a different contact so he could get his shirts made a more affordable price. We had many fantastic holidays after he made a few calls to is contacts to borrow a caravan for a week for very little or no cost. The best networking I experienced was when I arrived home from school and told him I had been selected to proceed onto week of work experience but now I just need to find a placement. He thought about it and the next day, he contacted one of his networks.

When he got home from work, he passed me a phone number and explained I needed to speak with Millie Hammersley. She was a local businesswoman who had a fantastic history as a Director both in business and football. She had recently opened a screen-printing business on one of the local industrial estates and had agreed to a placement for a week. I met Millie a few weeks later and she looked after me like a son – generously explaining the details of her business, customers, operations and finances. Every day at work was an immersion of the practicalities of business. I went on to secure a part-time job at the weekend which lasted for 3 years and after I had finished my A-levels, I worked at the printing plant for 5 months whilst waiting to join the Officer Training College at Royal Air Force Cranwell.

I've often thought about Dad's network and if I could help my children in the same way. I hope I could come up with some options for them, but it has been in my professional life I've really tried to follow in his footsteps. This has included securing employment through my network and when working for a business, building sufficient networks to be selected for projects.

Networks are a critical factor of personal and professional life enabling people to develop customers, create opportunities for learning, provide access to employment and give the chance to seize a short-term opportunity through the immediacy of a contact.

When to build a network

After my own early experience of networks in operation, I quickly learned to build a network before it is needed. This was reinforced in a book or article I read over 20 years ago. (Unfortunately, I cannot give the credit to the person who cemented this notion into my brain as I cannot find the article or book.)

What does this mean? If you're looking for a job or writing a book, it's too late to start trying to build a wide and varied network to help with content or referral to other people to help. What you've got now is what you're going to use. Some of the most successful people I have seen who have moved from corporate life into consulting have become successful as a solopreneur because of the networks they have built up over many years.

The ability to reach into a business to speak with a CHRO or CFO and avoid the gatekeeper is a competitive advantage that others will not have. If you're already thinking that you may need to build you own network, remember that for a network to be successful it must be mutually supportive. You can't have a successful network that is all one sided. We will discuss this in further detail within this chapter.

In 'The Tipping Point'[90], Gladwell tells the incredible story of the initial stages of the American War of independence where Paul Revere and William Dawes set out to warn the communities surrounding Boston that the British invasion was close. Both men set off at the same time, entering the same number of communities to spread the word that the British were coming. They rode on horseback throughout the night spreading the same message. Revere's discussions with his contacts, and the way he gave his message, resulted in drums, church bells and a rising of the people many miles away from where he had started his journey. Dawes' journey was not so successful. In fact, the British had so little opposition from the towns where Dawes had visited, they believed that they were pro-British. Revere had spoken to the network of revolutionary leaders and gained their support and trust so they raised an army. His success in connecting and messaging is a lesson for everyone and was achieved without modern day technology and on primitive roads. Imagine being able to state the outcomes that Revere achieved by accessing his network!

So, who is in your network on a professional basis? Stop for a few minutes to ask yourself this question. Identify the person/people you could go to for advice about your current role or to ask about a recommendation for a service provider. If you are struggling to do this, you may need to start to build a network now. If you are thinking of changing career or moving to a new part of country, start to reach out to people who can connect you with folks who are already where you want to be. Reaching out this way is building a network in advance of needing it. I have lived by this belief for many years and it has served me well.

How much effort on networking?

When you sign up for a conference, do you dread seeing the words 'networking opportunity'? I have spoken to senior leaders across a range of businesses and some have shrivelled up when I mention building a network. Like most people, they envisage forced networking sessions which achieve very little other than fear of any sort of networking in the future.

I attended a huge conference in London in 2018 – this one sticks in my memory! I had seen in the programme there was a 'networking opportunity' available at the close of the first day of the conference and as always, I wanted to make the most of the expensive ticket and investment in time. I entered the breakout room from the main conference hall to see around 200 people all being lined up by an over eager facilitator. We stood in two lines, each facing a stranger. When all the shuffling was over, we were told to speak to the person in front of us for 1 minute and then they could introduce themselves. After 2 minutes, a whistle was blown and we shuffled down 2 people. And so, it went on for what seemed like hours. It was hot. It was noisy. We could barely hear the person opposite and after a while, I started to tune into the conversations happening around me. At the end, the facilitator announced we had reached the end of the session and the bar was open. We all clapped and hurriedly left the room. I stood at the bar talking to 3 other people who had been in the session. Over the next hour, we all laughed off the networking experience and then learnt more about each other. Clearly, the organised networking was still no match for a casual conversation, with no pressure to get something out of it. Just what networking should be.

So, if you're one of many people who loathe the forced networking, I want you to know it's ok to feel like that. There maybe a few people who you really want to talk to but if all you get out of a networking event is a business card to set up an online meeting and have a proper discussion, then this is a great result. The trick is to build a network that is useful to you and this does not need to be thousands of people. 100 carefully selected contacts can be more powerful than 100,000 'followers' on Twitter that have been purchased over the internet. Networking through a process that is comfortable for you is more likely to be successful than a forced network through the conference breakout session that I attended.

As with most things in life, you get out of your network what you're prepared to put into it. The difficult part is building a network of people and you need to judge a few factors to maximise your time. How comfortable are you in walking into a room full of people you don't know and then striking up conversation?

How to build a network

We have 2 networks – face-to-face and online. For many people, the face-to-face networks are dwindling as we embrace more online tools in our work.

Regardless of the location of the network, there are some key things to remember:

- A professional network is different from your friends (although some friends may also be part of it).

- Your level of connectedness with your contacts will vary. Not everyone can be a top tier contact.

- Your network will change over time and you should seek to add more people to it.

- Your network is a great source of learning. For many of your contacts, this maybe your take-away.

- Don't approach a new contact with the expectation of an immediate return.

You should develop your own style of networking and then refine it as you learn from your mistakes! It's always good to observe how one of your trusted contacts builds their network. Every day I see this in operation on LinkedIn and some people are relentless. I've provided some ideas for building a network which is a mix of face-to-face and online contacts. You will need to amend some of these approaches given any specific cultural issues for your location or type of work:

- Making meaningful contact on a regular basis will lead to a more productive conversation.

- Approach a network contact with the view of 'how can I help them?' even if you are the one that needs their help.

- Talk about common connections or interests. You may find this provides more of an opportunity to get introduced to other people.

- Ask if you can introduce them to people, they are trying to connect to. They may offer the same help back.

- Don't think that forcing your way into a conversation and asking for a partnership, business, referral or investment is a cool way to network. This will only lead to rejection.

- If you get to meet in person, see if they are happy to share a photo on social media and tag each other into the post. This helps build a memory when you next speak to them.

To further build your network, look at who your network is connected to. In LinkedIn terms, who are your 2nd and 3rd degree contacts? This may provide the opportunity to connect with people who you may not normally get to meet. Equally, you can offer the introducer help with any introductions they may also need. For job seekers, this can be a great way to make an approach to a business where you want to work or for consultants, where you believe you can provide appropriate services.

I had the opportunity to speak with some amazing leaders on my podcast and ask them if they actively built their network.
Here are a selection of answers so you can see how leaders across the globe approach networking:

Jill Katz, Chief People Officer.

> *"I think the answer is yes and no. There is nothing more important than networking because, for me, that's how I learn. I'm learning by knowing you today, both of you and now you're going to be in my network. And after today you'll meet, you'll know someone that you think I should know. And by virtue of hearing that Andy knows this person and thinks I should know them, and that person will reach out and say, Andy Davies said that I should all talk to that person. And that, to me is the best way for all of us to learn and grow as people as humans as executives. And that is how I grow my network. I do have people reach out to me blind or cold. I've tried to personally accept as many as I can, where I believe I'll have the opportunity to learn something myself. I don't accept every single one, I certainly do not accept anything that's inappropriate. I think that's really important. Because unfortunately, that still happens. And as a female executive who takes her career very seriously, LinkedIn is not anything other than a place where I want to grow my career and my executive following. People that are sending me messages where I believe I'm going to learn something and gain something or maybe someone can learn something from me. I love to learn that way. But I'm certainly more interested in what I'm going to learn from you or someone that knows you. So, there's a personal connection. I also run my own virtual networking programme and I teach people how to network and I think that is my passion project. And that's called the Assemble network. That's a programme that I run on a monthly basis and we accept 12 people per month and each month is a separate private cohort."*

Mark Samlal, Founder and CEO, PayGroup Ltd.

> *"I am a relentless networker. I enjoy the interaction, I enjoy meeting the people. And whilst it's very stifled under these COVID times we do have tools such we're on today, Microsoft Teams, LinkedIn obviously, is a very important part of what I do. In terms of meeting people. I also recognise that networking in itself can't at all. So we pay for events, we attend webinars and other items like that, where you get to meet other industry leaders as well. And that's been a very big part of what we do. But knowing in my circle as it's expanded, who the right people are to come into your organisation in a external succession plan, as well as an internal succession plan is absolutely mandatory.*

You mentioned Chris Brunton before, I always wanted Chris to be able to work with Pay Asia and now Pay Group. But it also took me some time before was right. But he was always available for a chat. He was always available for a cup of coffee, he's always available to have a lunch with and just talk shop as well as talk as friends. Even well before the opportunity for him to join the group was and that was absolutely the same case with Frank when he was retiring from ADP and, as I say, went on his world tour to say goodbye to people. And I put him in a headlock and made him stay in Singapore for extra time to talk."

David James, Chief Learning Officer.

"It's a little bit of both. I think LinkedIn is amazing and has been amazing for growing network and a real network as well. Twitter has been amazing. The people who are active on Twitter, in the fields of HR and L&D are some of the most generous and insightful people I've ever met. People like Perry Tim's and dare and subscribe. And really prominent and really show that platform as a way of how would you How would you describe just being public? I just think I just think it could be a very real platform. at LinkedIn. I think he's useful. I was in the business of posting what could be seen as contentious posts, but really, it was just it was just thrown down the gauntlet to L&D a lot of the time. And you would make as many friends as you would enemies always. But the people who believed in that as well and become allies, and then the podcast really helps because I get an hour to chat with people that I never have spent that time with. I researched them I prepare a load of questions, we have a rich conversation, and then I remain in touch with them and afterwards as well. So it's kind of passive in the general day to day of what I do, but you could say that. But maybe it's because my working days engineered around connection."

Amy Jen Su, Managing Partner & Co-Founder.

"I think where I, one of my own biggest takeaways on this leadership journey, is that it truly takes a village, I do not, I cannot take credit for the experiences that I have, or where I am in this journey. It has been a multitude of people that I couldn't even begin to name that have made it possible. So I think your second question, it's been an and both where it's been largely organic. So we as an organisation have never done active marketing, we have been purely word of mouth, both the way we built our internal team and the way we built our client base, somebody somehow knew somebody that led to a wonderful referral or a door opening.

Or Andy, as you described how we had this lovely conversation on LinkedIn. And now we're having this wonderful conversation together. So that's the emergent part. And then I would say that I have also been intentional and conscious that when you're in the presence of good people, and you feel a shared mission, and you feel the synergy between you, I am pretty intentional about building and preserving relationship. So I think it's both allowing the universe if you will, to bring forward the people who are meant to be in your life, as much as it is be a good citizen of your network.

Don't just reach out to people when you need something, you know, have them in your mind, think about where the synergies are, and then be intentional. Who are the accountability buddies in your life? Or the helicopters? who bring you a special point of view or an aerial view? Who are your cheerleaders? Who are your safe harbours? And as you come to find those people, show them the due respect and thanks for the support they offer and be that for other people."

Beth Armknecht-Miller, Leadership Development Advisor & Coach

"If it's active in the way that I reach out to those people that that I am connected to, and, and, and ask for, you know, referrals and references to various people that that they know. Because if because if they know me and they know my work, they're going to represent me to that person that that they know. So, in fact, I've gotten two new clients in the last month through that method."

There will times when you are more passive in your networking. All it needs is a change of job or a new project and that can change in an instant. The leaders quoted above are currently driving business everyday so it's understandable that their responses are on the proactive side of the networking continuum. When you look around your friends, family or colleagues, consider their current approach to networking and what factors would be needed for them to shift from passive to active networking.

Case Study – Stepping out of a comfort zone

Gary Guwe – Director and Entrepreneur, Singapore
https://www.linkedin.com/in/garyguwe/

Jan began her career as a product coordinator at a fast-growing tech company in APAC. Jan is an extrovert who loves interacting with and engaging with people. She enjoys mathematics, travelling, learning and development, and volunteering her time as a parent at her children's school to help improve their learning experience of the students there.

Jan also believes in challenging herself by immersing herself in different projects and learning from them; she is ambitious, determined, resourceful and resilient – and is focused on seeking progression in her career at her company.

Jan understands that she will not only need to perform well in her role as a product coordinator. To stand out, she'll need to be visible and have allies who would help her in her role. Where information from a department is hard to come by, Jan is able to tap on her network to access the necessary insights and information necessary to make decisions that are critical to the success of the projects she's spearheading.

Where it comes to going above and beyond and delivering even more value, Jan is able to hold her own when it comes to meetings with her client and the sales team. She's able to quickly and effectively read and engage with her client(s), and engage with them on topic that they care about, i.e.: parenting challenges, travelling and saving time to do the things they enjoy.

Small talk aside, Jan asks great questions and is able to quickly identify and diagnose the challenges her clients want resolved; her clients appreciate that Jan is always on point, and that meetings with her are both enjoyable and efficient – and that they are able to address their key concerns effectively with Jan in those meetings.

To build and sharpen her leadership and people management capabilities, Jan also volunteers and leads office events like the annual Christmas/Dinner and Dance, and Mental Health & Wellness Day. Her role(s) in leading and organizing events like these provides her with the unique opportunity and access to engage with and interact with the company executives and leaders, as well as other members from other departments across the company. Coupled with her quarterly involvement hosting the company townhall meetings, Jan is not only able to sharpen her communication and presentation skills, but also raise her profile within the company in APAC.

After a year on the job, Jan has firmly established herself as an important asset and talent in the company. She is highly visible and known to both her peers within and outside her department, and is recognized by the company's leadership for her contributions to the company beyond her formal job profile.
Her organizational abilities are well-known, and she is widely perceived to possess the potential to shoulder even more responsibilities with the company.

Jan's work results and excellent client testimonials, organizational and people management abilities places her on the fast-track to winning a promotion to junior manager within a year and a half on the job.

Despite being a junior manager, Jan now has 9 direct reports under her charge, and leads one of the biggest sub-division in her department at the company.

Gary's case study of Jan shows her way of networking and spending time with executives and other people across departments. This case study is focused on internal networking which is often overseen. Although you may be in the same business, there is a requirement to build networks before you need them both internally and externally.

Does a leader need a social media network?

I want to turn my attention away from 'in-person' networking and examine social media networks. They are both different and the same from face-to-face networking. Social media makes people available. Often, this is the unintended consequence of sharing information on social media and can bring more challenges than expected. You are open to challenge and negative feedback. You can easily give your competitors information that they may have not known or it could have taken them many months to discover.

If I look at my LinkedIn contacts, I am connected to CEOs of billion-pound businesses and I can send them a message. Even if I'm not directly connected to them, I can tag people into posts along with their business and indirectly communicate with them.

When I'm advertising for a job within my team, I can access my network on both LinkedIn and Twitter to reach a wide audience. Maybe the job isn't directly for them, but if they re-share it with their networks, I start to access more candidates than I could do on my own. My openness on these platforms means that people can contact me and discuss future business opportunities, ask about future employment or seek guidance/mentorship. My customers can contact me directly or my global partners can quickly connect me to their potential customers.

As you're already aware, there are a myriad of social media platforms that can be used for professional networking: LinkedIn, Twitter, Instagram, Facebook etc. Each has its own area of strength and it's wrong to say that the post on one platform will gain the same response as another. The great aspect of social media networks is that everyone is different. I've had people approach me (online and in person) to advise that I'm doing it wrong and I don't understand social media. I don't spend too much time with these folks as there is no defined route for being successful as a leader who is available on social media.

What every leader needs to develop is digital confidence. Just as you are confident in sending an email to a colleague or presenting to a meeting, leaders need to develop their confidence around social media platforms. Posting should be effortless but still contain thought about what is being posted as this immediately sets the tone for your personal brand. At first, it's difficult and you will over-analyse the words you are about to post. This concern is entirely normal and you will grow your confidence the more you do this.

There is a fantastic book I'd like to recommend to all leaders; it's *Known* by Mark Schaefer and is listed in the further reading for this chapter. I read this book at the beginning of my own social media journey and there are so many useful points that I have kept at the forefront of my mind since reading *Known*. Mark was a guest on my podcast and we talked about how the book gripped me and he acknowledged that he had received the same feedback from many other readers. This book is a great reference for any leader to learn more about social media.

There is a great risk of leaders being left behind if they do not have a social media network. It's not just about FOMO (Fear of Missing Out) it is bigger than that. Across the web, more providers are setting up their own networking groups and sites to support greater networking. (The lure of marketing revenue also helps motivate some providers but let's not tarnish everyone with that approach.)

Forbes[91] established 'Forbes Connect' in 2020 which is aimed at the c-suite and "will provide reliable content on business, leadership, and strategy via the Forbes CEO vertical and influential lists".[92] This is supported by a range of events and is an example of passively building a network. I've had the pleasure of being part of some great networks including #HRHour, my local CIPD Branch and the Business Development Society in Singapore. There are many opportunities for networking and sometimes you just need to find them!

Social media networks – links to stakeholders

In 2017, Paul Franks tweeted Elon Musk with the following:

Paul Franks
@pjfranks1509

@elonmusk can you guys program the car once in park to move back the seat and raise the steering wheel? Steering wheel is wearing.

1:47 AM · Aug 19, 2017 from Bamford, AL · Twitter for iPad

76 Retweets 14 Quote Tweets 1,718 Likes

Elon Musk @elonmusk · Aug 19, 2017
Replying to @pjfranks1509
Good point. We will add that to all cars in one of the upcoming software releases.
266 578 8.4K

As everyone knows, Elon is a big Twitter fan, constantly giving updates on his products and sometimes getting into trouble for his announcements. On this occasion, just 24 minutes later, Elon responded with "Good point. We will add that to all cars in one of the upcoming software releases." Here's a great example of a CEO engaging directly with his customers to listen to feedback which will make his product more appealing to his growing customer base.

As a piece of marketing, it's genius. In 16 words, he has achieved more exposure of Telsa and forthcoming enhancements that would otherwise have taken time and cost through a marketing agency. 3 years on from this tweet, we're still talking about it and the impact.

Now, in this example, Elon is not connected to Paul as part of a formal network. It is the informal social media network that has brought them together as Paul was able to access Elon through Twitter.
Social media is an incredibly powerful opportunity for customers to have available CEOs and other leaders of global businesses. Equally, it is powerful for leaders to be available to their customers and other stakeholders through social media. Global giants such as Tesla, and a leader who is social media aware, can easily address issues, receive feedback, generate sales and increase marketing.

There are many reasons for you to be social media aware and use it as part of your networking strategy:

- Authentic conversations without a filter or gatekeeper.

  It cannot be underestimated how much people hate leaders who are not authentic. Putting on a show and following a script will not build a network. Second on this list of hated items is the gatekeeper who protects and deflects people from getting close to a leader. Social media enables leaders to connect. Really connect. In the moment and at scale.

- Faster turnaround on feedback or questions you want to ask.

  This is where you don't want to have someone manage your social media accounts for you. Phil Foden, an English footballer, recently sacked his social media account management company after they posted an inflammatory comment on his behalf to an opposing player.[93] You need to own your content and answer questions yourself – your social media management company can't be authentic on your behalf.

- Social media networks can work for you 24/7 in all regions.

  I've worked across EMEA, APAC and the US dealing with enquiries from all regions in the same day. I have a presence in many local networks and have actively built these to support sales and channel partnerships. Social media networks help me do this when I'm not there.

- Valuable insights into competitors and customers.

  Don't underestimate the power of a few lines about your competitors or seeing that one of their executives have moved on. Your customers also will give more away about your competitors as they look for new suppliers and provide updates on why they are switching suppliers.

- Spot opportunities to help contacts within your network.

  I celebrate the opportunity to help my network especially when I can see that someone is looking for a new job. There is a chance I can help the person seeking new employment and another contact who has just posted a vacancy.

- Source talent, both passive and active, for your business.

  Sometimes those folks who are looking for a new job might also be a perfect fit for my business! The network I have also give me an opportunity to reach out to some passive candidates and ask if they have time for a discussion about a forthcoming role. If this doesn't work out with the initial approach, they might be willing to direct me to other people who may be interested.

- Show that you have interests outside of work.

  This isn't just about pictures of me skiing in France. You will also build a more diverse network of people given your other interests including voluntary work, trustee of a charity, youth leader (Scouts or Guides) or pro-bono work for specific charities.

Before you to start posting on random social media apps, here are some things to consider:

- Select the right platform for what you are trying to achieve.

Not all social media platforms are the same. What's your primary content that you want to share? Who are the people who will consume your content that you want to network with? Is your focus on securing interim jobs or employment? There are hundreds of social media apps that are designed for discussions, sharing, contacting friends, networking, hosting groups, news, sports, entertainment. The choice you make will affect the network you can build. Talk to others in your network to see what they use and research on the web to find the most suitable. If you make a mistake with this choice, you will waste time repeating your efforts to build a network on a new platform.

- Decide on who is your audience and post accordingly for them.

  This links in with choosing the right platform. Your content defines you and will attract the audience it is appropriate for. Whilst remaining your authentic self, make sure you know who you wish to connect with and write accordingly.

- Consider how you wish to be seen online.

  How do you wish to be seen online? Remember that what you post now will be brought up in years to come – possibly when you're applying for a job. Former CEO of VisuWell, Sam Johnson[94], was terminated after a video was posted on twitter showing him harassing a gay teen in a dress at a prom in 2021. If this is your authentic self, then you will get found out.

- Consider your picture and profile carefully.

  Your personal brand is key. You may need to think about the cultural norms where you work and how you wish to be seen in that locale. I've worked with people who have always had their signature item of clothing so people would remember them. One lady had an enormous collection of silk scarves and would wear a different bow every day. Another colleague decided that bow ties would be his standout item that he wore as often as possible.

- Decide on your approach to building a network. Passive or active?

  How active are you going to be in building a network? I see Sales Executives reaching out to announce they're in a new role and now want to connect with senior people in an industry. I appreciate what they are trying to achieve but it comes across as desperate and they may as well start their email with "I've got to hit my first month target to pass my probation can you help me?". Alternatively, you can sit back and see what happens and who finds your profile. I'm not a fan of either approach as a network should be curated.

- What are you going to post and how often?

  Finding your own level in the use of your chosen platform is again part of your brand as people will soon get to know who they see commenting on every new post and asking for people to connect. You can easily source 10 pieces of content to share with your network. But to help establish yourself as a trusted expert, 2-3 pieces with considered analysis of the content and involving your contacts in the discussion will be better accepted by your network.

- Do you have a personal hashtag that you wish to use consistently?

  Hashtags have grown in prominence since their first use in Twitter in 2007 and are a way of categorising your posts. Across many platforms you can easily search for content based on a hashtag. I recently started using #leadershipfailure on LinkedIn to help me categorise the cases I wanted to use in this book - have a look and see if I'm in your results! To understand the power of social media in more depth, I want to refer you to *Known* by Mark Schaefer which I have already mentioned. If you want to know more about building your presence then this is the book you need to read.

Social media networks – thought leadership

Are you a leader in your market? Some folks have turned their social media presence into an opportunity to position themselves as a thought leader in their domain. This takes networking to a new level and moves away from the more personalised network of deeply understood contacts to a 'numbers matter' game. Who are thought leaders?

Depending on your interest, everyone will have a different answer. Here are some of the thought leaders I follow and think of when this topic is raised:

- Ariana Huffington – https://www.linkedin.com/in/ariannahuffington/
- Simon Sinek – https://www.linkedin.com/in/simonsinek/
- Josh Bersin – https://www.linkedin.com/in/bersin/
- Dave Ulrich – https://www.linkedin.com/in/daveulrichpro/
- Meghan Biro - https://www.linkedin.com/in/meghanmbiro/
- Adam Grant – https://www.linkedin.com/in/adammgrant/

- Dan Pink - https://www.linkedin.com/in/danielpink/

Recently, I saw a post from a well-known author and I like their work; I've read their books and I have worked with them. They explained how they and their team (!) have recently grown their LinkedIn followers to over 50,000. This has now transcended normal networking as this person is looking to position themselves as a thought leader to achieve marketing revenue for articles, videos, webinars or through the sale of their consultancy services. I'm telling you this because I want you to consider how you feel about this. Do you think it is authentic? Or is it just business?

The downside of social media networks

The previous example where Elon responded to his customer about his feedback on the Telsa steering wheel is a great example of how to positively use social media to help you and your network. Unfortunately, as Elon discovered, it can also be the source of many issues. In May 2020, as Covid19 was gripping the world, Elon tweeted:

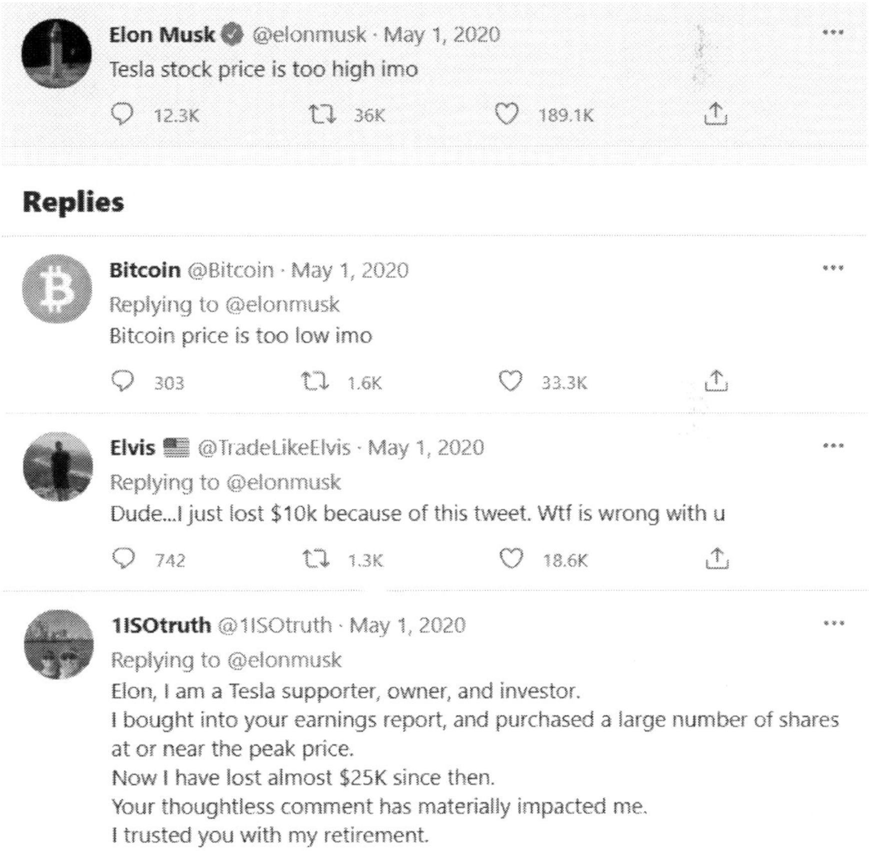
Elon Musk @elonmusk · May 1, 2020
Tesla stock price is too high imo
12.3K 36K 189.1K

Replies

Bitcoin @Bitcoin · May 1, 2020
Replying to @elonmusk
Bitcoin price is too low imo
303 1.6K 33.3K

Elvis @TradeLikeElvis · May 1, 2020
Replying to @elonmusk
Dude...I just lost $10k because of this tweet. Wtf is wrong with u
742 1.3K 18.6K

1ISOtruth @1ISOtruth · May 1, 2020
Replying to @elonmusk
Elon, I am a Tesla supporter, owner, and investor.
I bought into your earnings report, and purchased a large number of shares at or near the peak price.
Now I have lost almost $25K since then.
Your thoughtless comment has materially impacted me.
I trusted you with my retirement.

Unsurprisingly, this caused a flurry of responses from investors (his wider network) who were able to calculate the impact of these words. Elon faced further challenges as the Stock Exchange Commission considered if this was a breach of a previous infringement from 2018 where he had previously made a claim about funding for a private buyout of Tesla. Just to compound the issue, a shareholder[95] then filed a lawsuit against Elon for this tweet and the impact it had on the share price. The outcome is that the Tesla share price rose dramatically raising the questions, is there ever such a thing as bad publicity?

Part of the challenges faced by social media users is the immediacy of the post. In the moment, a tweet or post can be posted and then it is too late. In the past, we have all sent an email and then tried to recall it. This never really worked as it simply highlighted to the recipient that you wanted to recall an email which made them more curious about reading it. Social media has more immediate and with a wider reach. For people to represent their business on a platform, they need to understand their boundaries and how to deal with difficult situations.

At the start of my social media journey, I spent time building my Twitter network using many of the pieces of advice I have provided so far. Reaching out to business leaders and HR leaders through online groups and following them on Twitter. Everything was going to plan or even easier than I had expected. I released a Tweet about an article I had posted online and received a scathing comment. It was from a senior leader with a large Twitter following. He was known for being a bit bullish and when I took part in online networking events, he always seemed to be controversial for the sake of it. My initial reaction was anger. How dare he post such a comment! I started to type a response and it wasn't a great set of words! Fortunately, before I pressed send, I realised that all my contacts I had worked so hard to build were about to see this tweet. I deleted the text and ignored Twitter for 24 hours.

The following day, I spent some time thinking how I was going to respond to this comment. It had bugged me during the night. I thought about contacting him directly. The more options I assessed, the more unsure I became about how this might work out. So I started to type. "Thanks for your comment." Once I had pressed send, I was free. I had dealt with the most difficult part of my social networking and I had gone through the mental anguish of where my own boundary lines existed. There are many other tactics I have employed over the years. One successful tactic is to do nothing. This allows time for others to add comments which then dilute the impact of the original negative comment and on many occasions, other contributors will call out the troll. People will post on social media comments that they would never say in person. Trolling exists for weak people so don't fuel their fire.

Since that first negative comment, I've received several other comments that warranted the same response. I'm no longer de-railed by the varying opinions I receive about my articles or posts. There is always the ultimate sanction. I have blocked 5 people on LinkedIn/Twitter because of their comments on my posts. One was promoting racist views and the other 4 used profanities in their comments.

Each one of these experiences has helped me to determine further boundaries but the person I blocked for a racist comment was the most difficult. I had worked with him some years ago. We had gone our separate ways as I headed off for an overseas secondment and we had only briefly bumped into each other on one occasion. He wasn't a friend. He was an acquaintance. This was the most important lesson for me as I had learned that any contact in my network can be removed.

Networking on social media gives a wider target to aim for within your industry and across national boundaries. However, to be successful at it you need to find your own levels of comfort and expect that you will have a bumpy ride at some point.

Summary

You are in control of your network and you are responsible for having a network in place before you need it. If you're still wondering if this is for you, consider a small piece of research conducted by Professor Uzzi[96] from Kellogg School of Management. He surveyed 280 sales executives about their networks and how they had impacted their professional lives. 57% said that networking had resulted in a 'large' impact on their career. Whilst looking at their sales results, a sales rep who placed a high value on their network attributed 36% of their sales to their network. For the sales rep who had placed a low value on their network, they only attributed 6% of their sales to their network.

As I have already described, I have been fortunate enough to secure two roles through my network. On one occasion I had arranged a start date for my next engagement 3 days before I had finished at the previous engagement simply because I had announced to my network that I would be available for work the following week.

But the important element of my network is being able to introduce people to each other who may be able to help each other. I have done this on countless occasions and generated business for others in the process. You can now decide on what is important to you about your network and how you can use the many opportunities you are provided with to help your network.

If you want to know what everyone is doing about their networks, I asked 100 people within my network who are based globally in many different sectors. Here are the results:

- Actively build my network – 49%

- Passively build my network - 9%
- Occasional interest in growth - 25%
- Let it sort itself out - 16%

This research shows that nearly half of the leaders surveyed actively seek to grow their network and this boosted to three quarters of all leaders when an occasional growth is taken into account. For those that have a no interest in the growth of their network, they are in the minority (16 people). In simple terms, your leadership peers are growing their network and they will be able to connect with more people for business opportunities than leaders who show little interest in their network. If you've not started to nurture your network, now is the time.

Reflective activities

- Complete the assessment tool in 'Social Chemistry' to understand if you are an expansionist, broker or convener.

- Consider how you network and how you will network in the future. Write down actions to take for building your network, giving something back to you network, how you can use social media to network, what type of people do you wish to network with and who in your network will you speak to about the growth of their network?

- Review your network. Is this primarily internal or external contacts? If you have an imbalance, determine a way to redress the imbalance.

Suggested reading

- King M. (2020). *Social Chemistry*. London: Hodder and Stoughton.

- Schaefer M. (2017). *Known*. USA: Schaefer.

Chapter 10

Future leadership

"We need to accept that we don't always make the right decisions, that we'll screw up royally sometimes. Understand that failure is not the opposite of success, it's part of success."
Arianna Huffington (CEO of Thrive Global)

Introduction

The way we lead has changed forever. The old structures which included command and control were arrangements put in place in the industrial revolution to help business owners see that everyone was at work and being productive. People were treated as a commodity to be traded and worked until they could no longer meet the performance standard and they were replaced. Employee experience was irrelevant, communication was through barked orders and understanding of a vision was zero. People worked to stay alive.

We now have employees who are informed about global events and markets. They have a mobile phone which connects them to shifting news articles. Many people are more understanding of the business environment they work in than the leaders of the same business. People have choice. This choice is not just limited to their local community but across the globe as they have the freedom to move or simply conduct remote working for a business on a different continent.

In 2020, Iceland ran trials covering 1.3 per cent of the Icelandic[97] workforce which revealed that a 4-day week led to better employee wellbeing, while productivity stayed the same or improved. The positive results sparked union pressure in Iceland, and now 86% of Icelandic workers either work shorter weeks or have the right to ask to do so. Pressure is mounting on businesses and leaders to do more for their workers to maintain a healthy balance between their personal and work lives.

The opportunity for our people to be freed from repetitive and monotonous tasks is supported through increased technology and connectivity. Our leaders will need a different way of supporting people than before. If there has been a seismic shift in our focus on our people since the industrial revolution, we now need to go through the same level of shift again but with a clear focus on how technology and connectivity are going to shape the way we lead.

This chapter will cover how the changes in the external environment and technology should affect your thinking as a leader and offer a blueprint for success as a future leader.

The external environment

I have mentioned that a leader has the responsibility to scan the external environment for threats and opportunities for their business. This advice is not a hollow statement and it should be treated as a key piece of advice to all future leaders.

The external threats to businesses occur in many forms including increased competition (existing rivals, new entrants, substitutes, merger and acquisitions), access to resources, access to finance, changes to legislation, global crisis (war, pandemic etc) and changes in technology to name a few.

Until September 2021, how many of the British public realised the importance of CO^2 in the production of food? The rising gas prices had caused CF Industries[98], a major producer of CO^2 in the UK, to shut down its plants as the rising gas price had made it uneconomical to run their plants in Teeside and Cheshire. In this example, it is not the rising gas prices that should be the focus. What efforts were the leaders of the businesses that were reliant on their CO^2 doing to monitor the external environment and the subsequent rises in the cost of gas? Whilst food producers were the people in the press highlighting the issue, the lack of CO^2 also hit hospitals, the nuclear industry and fire extinguisher manufacturers. This example is a case of monitoring the environment for threats to the resources that are key to the operation of a business.

The first Blockbuster[99] store opened in Dallas in 1985. It grew to a franchise of over 9,000 stores, employed over 84,000 people and was once valued at $3 billion. At its peak in the 90s it earned more than $800 million in late fees alone. In the late 90s Blockbuster entered discussions with Enron over a video-streaming service which led Enron to build and test a successful video-streaming platform. However, Blockbuster pulled out of the deal in 2001 so they could focus on their core video hire shops. During the time Blockbuster and Enron had been playing with the idea of a video-streaming platform, Reed Hastings had established Netflix in a response to being charged $40 from Blockbuster for a late return fee.

Instead of the need to go to a physical store, Netflix would post out DVDs with a pre-paid return envelope – no late return fees! Blockbuster failed to notice the external environment was changing and so were their customers. Younger customers who were more tech savvy wanted a different approach to rent their films. The last Blockbuster film was rented on 9 November 2013 and this brought a close to a business that had once made millions but now had filed for bankruptcy with a $900 million debt.

Technology

Between 2013-2019, Amazon increased its use of robots from 1,000 to 200,000[100]. In 2016, SpaceX performed the first successful landing of a rocket onto an Autonomous Spaceport Drone Ship[101]. Since 2015, Starship Technologies have been using miniature autonomous vehicles to deliver food to around 200,000 people in Milton Keynes. In 2020, Skyports carried out a trial in Argyll and Bute with drones to deliver PPE and Covid19 testing kits to people in the remote islands of Scotland transforming a 6-hour journey into a 15 minute on-demand service. In 2021, John Deere[102] announced that it would acquire Bear Flag Robotics, a Silicon Valley start-up that makes fully autonomous tractors for farms, for $250 million.

What have you done to challenge the use of technology in your business to increase the customer experience and drive the competitive advantage you have? If the answer is you have not done anything, then you should be concerned for the future of your business. Throughout the business world, your competitors are seeking to use technology to drive their business forward. Even businesses you currently do not consider to be your competition are only a few steps away from developing rival products or substitutes that will undermine your business. And in most cases, this is driven using technology. PWC have researched the impact of this use of technology and noted that 37% of people are worried about automation putting jobs at risk - up from 33% in 2014[103].

I have seen the incredible changes in the workforce in many countries. This has been driven by the accelerating growth of technology in all areas of our lives including work. I have run HR offices which were paper-based where we had one terminal to process all the forms once a week. At one point, part of my role was to be the system administrator for our HR, payroll and finance system which involved receiving a tape through the post to update the software three times a year. As time has progressed, I have had the pleasure of introducing thousands of people to the joy of employee self-service and watched as HR teams celebrated the immediate cessation of paper-based claims.

In hindsight, I joined the workforce at the start of the current technology revolution and a lot of my HR career has been supporting digital transformation across all areas of HR. When I speak with other HR pros some HR and payroll teams are still struggling with outdated processes and without the tech that is designed to remove the manual effort and move these professionals to more value adding activities. I still work with people who have grown a business to over 1000 people and still operate every function of HR through a spreadsheet. The thought of this is frightening for several varied reasons including GDPR, data security, corrupt files, malicious actions/honest mistakes, lack of backups to name but a few.

Take 2 minutes to ask yourself, what jobs can you imagine in the future that have not been invented yet? I asked this on LinkedIn which sparked a discussion both on and offline. Here are some of the proposals:

- Autonomous Taxi Air Controller (my own suggestion).
- Gig Economy Counsellor.
- Curator of Apple Devices at the Smithsonian.
- Director of Remote Worker Wellbeing. (The survey was done pre-Covid19 but how insightful!)
- Social assimilation coach - programs built to teach human interaction for those who are over digitized.
- Virtual Reality Integration Coach.

Here is what the job advert for the Autonomous Taxi Air Controller might look like and it may be closer than you think:

Figure 10.1 – Advert for a future job

Autonomous Taxi Air Controller
Firebird Airspace – Staffordshire

A new and exciting position has arisen for an Autonomous Taxi Air Controller within our transport division of Firebird Airspace. This position requires an enthusiastic person with high levels of attention to detail to join our newly formed team in Hanley. You must possess a positive attitude and a proactive approach that ensures we deliver on time.

Working Hours: Home based, 40 hrs per week

Location: Hanley

Salary: £43,000

Controlling state of the art technology, you will provide a safe environment for all autonomous taxis in the Staffordshire airspace. This will include close monitoring of a fleet of 100 vehicles with over 300 journeys per hour and this may require alerting authorities to any unforeseen incidents. Reacting to any in-vehicle emergency communications in a calm manner may also be necessary. You will be fully supported by our detailed induction and continuous training programme through the Civil Aviation Authority.

Key Responsibilities

- *Monitor all autonomous vehicle movements in Staffordshire.*
- *Take immediate action in the case of emergency.*

- *Liaise with passengers who may have encountered a situation.*
- *Reporting any near misses to the Civil Aviation Authority.*

If you are engaged in a business which relies on people to process information, then the chances are this will all be replaced by robots in the next 5 years. According to Finance101[104] the top jobs to be automated include finance clerks, secretarial and administrative assistants and cashiers. If you are business relies on these roles, then now is the time to start looking for technology to replace these costly services.

Doing nothing

You have probably been taught that when conducting an options study, one of the options should be 'do nothing'. There are always pros and cons of the 'do nothing' option and many people will look to take this option as it allows them to continue as they have been doing for many years before.

Real leaders will look at all options and seldom do nothing. Even making minor changes to the people, processes or technologies may provide some improvement in a situation. I attended the Royal Air Force College at Cranwell as a young Officer Cadet and took part in a training exercise in the first few weeks after joining. It was my turn to lead the team. We got to the end of the exercise where the instructor provided a debrief on my performance.

After the team had all given their feedback, she turned to me and said, "You failed to make a decision." She was right. At a critical point in the exercise I had the opportunity to make a 50/50 decision and I did nothing. Events overtook me and I was forced down a route that I had not planned for. My lesson from this was any decision would have been better than do nothing. I could have at least defended the decision I made and planned for some activity to support it. Instead, I put myself in an unwinnable situation where I was constantly reacting to events and no time for proactivity. I have not made this mistake since that day.

As future leaders, you need to lead. By seizing the moment and making a decision, you will be ahead of the leaders who have chosen to do nothing. I have already discussed the need for bravery as a leader and this should help you understand why and when this is required. You will be presented with this problem on many occasions during your career and you can determine your success by your willingness to make a decision and act.

You must then remain agile enough to flex your route through a problem.

Blueprint for future leaders

The previous sections should help you reflect on how you plan for changes to your business including external factors and the impact of technological change. Whilst these are important, you should look to gain knowledge of all aspects of your internal business so you are aware of how changes externally will affect the business.

This will mean arranging secondments or shadowing opportunities so you can understand how you and your team contribute to the vision and goals of the business.

To accelerate your progress, you should focus on the 13 key success factors for a leader. I have identified these through bitter experience, research and discussions with business leaders throughout my career. You may wish to add others to this list from your own experience:

Figure 10.2 – Blueprint for leadership

Competence

You must be able to measure yourself and other leaders against an agreed set of competencies that support the future of your business. As a leader of the future, you need to have the competence required to deliver leadership in the future not leadership that was required in the past.

Approach

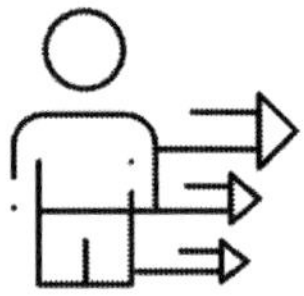

Your leadership approach needs to reflect the changing workforce and how people expect to be led. Explore the discovery questions in Chapter 3 to baseline your integrity, understanding of yourself, the people around you and your impact. Consider who are your role models and make conscious decision about how you will act. Seeking feedback will hone your approach and help you learn faster.

Networking

Linked closely to social selling is the need for you to network extensively. If your network is limited to just the people you work with, it has no use for external influence and reach. Build your network actively and frequently focusing on quality over quantity. The more authentic you are the more success you will have.

Marketplace

Where is your marketplace? The multi-channel marketplace is still a relatively new concept for some businesses. Are you still focused on direct sales through a recruited sales team when your competitors are using direct, online and partner channels? How can you react quickly to develop a presence on a new marketplace?

Social selling

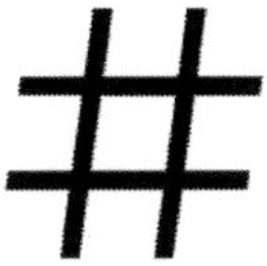

Have you built your online brand to ensure you have influence with your connections so when you post or comment it is noticed? Social media is a powerful route into your customer base and you should have a voice in these areas. As an expert in your service or product, you should be heard and role modelling the behaviour you seek from your own team.

Communication

Learn how to communicate. Communication is not a competence that is delivered with a title and takes time to master. Communicate widely and frequently but ensure you listen to what you are told. Communication is not just a licence to broadcast your views but a time to listen carefully to what your team has to tell you.

Culture

You should start by understanding what your culture is as perceived by current employees, previous employees and prospective employees. Once you have a rounded view of what your culture is you can then seek to influence it. In Chapter 6 I provided 9 elements of culture which may help you to frame the understanding of your culture. Great leader will always care about their culture and be transparent about the need to change a culture that is not productive.

Change

Your ability to lead change will be required through your years of leadership. The need to lead change does not dimmish with a promotion, indeed it is required more. Great leaders will make transformative changes whilst average

leaders will make transactional changes. Such change is a key area to embrace and drive change within a business.

Customer

Your focus should be on your customers as they are the ones paying for your services or products. Great leaders have a focus on customers and the commercial situation of their business, regardless of which department they lead. If you do not have regular access to customers, it is your job to seek and create opportunities to speak with customers and hear about their experience with your business.

Mobility

Be prepared to act with agility to meet the demands of your customers and your business. Your speed to react to opportunities and threats locally, nationally and internationally will make you stand out from other leaders. This may require some planning to ensure you can travel when required but this effort will be rewarded when you can act quicker than your competitors.

Talent

Posting a job vacancy on a job board and setting a deadline date will not get you the talented people you are looking for. Those days are gone. You need to seek out the talent you require and nurture it, sometimes for many months before they are ready to discuss. Look for the less obvious routes to communicating with a talent pool and seek to appoint for people with the right attitude.

Development

Are you continually learning or have you decided you have learnt enough? If you are not prepared to continually develop your own skills and knowledge, you cannot support the development of you team. A great leader will seek out opportunities to learn and support their team in developing into future leaders.

Bravery

Never be afraid to take on a project where others have failed. These projects offer an opportunity to achieve a great result and project your profile. Be prepared to stop a project if it is not going well and reset the understanding, vision and goals with a team. Showing bravery in these circumstances will set you apart from other leaders.

If you have mastered these success factors and focused you time on developing others, how many high performers can you identify within your team? A leader should be committed to developing other leaders. You can only do this by being the best leader you can be so that others can follow your example and learn from your mistakes.

The future of work and leadership

Leaders and future leaders are working in a challenging time brought about by continual technological change, increased mobility of a changing workforce and constantly evolving markets. This provides an opportunity for leaders to lead their teams through adversity and ambiguity. What is required for this is *Zest*. This energy is an exciting component of leadership that is often seen as refreshing. As a new or upcoming leader, you should already possess a Zest that others may have lost through cynicism and you have a chance to use this to motivate both yourself and others. Your energy can drive you to explore new avenues, to be brave when running pilot schemes and then lead transformation leadership that others are unable to do.

Do you have that *Zest*?

Reflective activities

- Review the key success factors and consider your approach to these factors in your working life. Speak to others and ask them for their view about your delivery of these factors!

- Consider how you can use your energy and *Zest* to bring change and motivate others?

- As a leader, how will you work with other leaders that have lost their energy and *Zest* without alienating them?

Suggested reading

- Morgan J. (2014). *The future of work*. Wiley. New Jersey.

Chapter 11

Leadership creed

Creed - a set of beliefs or aims which guide someone's actions

For most leaders, when they started out nobody sat them down and really explained how to behave and what to do. The context in which you lead will change throughout your career and will be driven by location, demands of the business, local culture and your own personal circumstances.

I know this because I was one of those leaders! It takes time, experience and mistakes to determine your own leadership creed. The other difficulty is this will change with time – do not be fooled into thinking there is one fixed way to lead as that is a guarantee of failure.

Additionally, trying to write down your own leadership creed is difficult. You should see this as a challenge that makes you think, reflect and agonise about what it means to you. This is incredibly personal and whilst there may be similarities with other people's leadership creeds, yours will always be unique to you because of who you are.

Here is a leadership creed to help provide a basis for your leadership which is taken from the chapters within this book. You can add and amend this creed as your leadership experience grows but this will always be here as your reference.

- I will constantly develop myself and support others to develop themselves.
- I will develop leaders of the future.
- I will seek to serve my team by providing the resources they need to be successful.
- I will lead with charisma and authenticity.
- I will learn how not to lead from the poor leaders around me.
- I will own all my decisions.
- I will embrace the opportunity that change brings.
- I will communicate regularly and with transparency.

- I will build a culture that enables people to be proud of their work.
- I will lead change and be a role model for change whilst considering the impact on people around me.
- I will focus on the customer experience and seek feedback from customers.
- I will trust and empower my team to deliver the vision and goals.
- I will build my network in advance of needing it.
- I will seek to learn from people around me.
- I will acknowledge when I am wrong.
- I will say 'thank you' and recognise when people have delivered beyond expectation.
- I will build a diverse team and embrace different viewpoints.
- I will constantly review how I can be a better leader.

Add your additions to the leadership creed here:

- I will ____
- I will ____
- I will ____
- I will ____

Now it's over to you to provide the leadership for the future generation of leaders.

Acknowledgements

I want to start by saying thanks to all the leaders who I have learned something from. This includes those I have worked with, those I have observed, the leaders who have gone out of their way to teach me and all the leaders I have read about during my research. And a big shout out to those leaders who failed which also allowed me to learn! These have been the greatest lessons of all.

Firstly, to all of the Scout leaders who taught me so much in my formative years, I thank you. I had the pleasure of meeting some incredible leaders who gave their time freely to share knowledge, skills and build my confidence that I would carry to every job I ever had. These Scout leaders were unsung heroes, and it took me a long time to realise that I learnt so much from their leadership skills as they motivated, inspired, mentored and showed trust in so many young people. I hope they realise their impact on the development of future leaders. I will be donating 20% of any profits from this book to 5th Stone St Michael Scout Group.

Case study authors – I appreciate your time to compose and edit your case studies until we were both happy with the outcome. You really have given your time to this book and I hope you get excited by showing your friends and family your contribution. These wonderful people are: Iain Fraser, Gary Guwe, Deborah Hartung and Hiten Bhatt.

Deborah Hartung – We've had some incredible discussions and I have learned a lot from, especially about the working environment and culture in South Africa. Thanks for helping me expand my global knowledge and meet your network on a different continent. Another fantastic panelist on 'Leadership, the future and tea'.

Hiten Bhatt – I love our conversations where you inspire to achieve more. Your faith drives you to be the amazing person you are and I have the pleasure of working with you. Thanks for energising me when I lost the drive to complete this book.

Julie Hodges – Thanks for giving me the chance to contribute a case study to your book around 5 years ago and our subsequent conversations where you have encouraged me to write this book. It was great seeing your process of writing and gain the confidence that I could do something similar.

Rebecca Carter, Iain Fraser & Anne McKinlay - Thanks for your help!

Cathy Davies, for all the editing and morale support throughout the processes, I could not have done this without you.

Imje Tse Publishing – Thanks to my publishers for showing trust and commitment in me with writing Zest. I really appreciate your support and hope to work with you on my next book.

Connect and network

Join me on LinkedIn:

Follow me on Twitter:

Visit my website for resources, links to recommended books and more information about upcoming projects:

[1] https://www.cia.gov/news-information/featured-story-archive/2012-featured-story-archive/simple-sabotage.html
[2] Colonna J. (2019). *Reboot: Leadership and the Art of Growing Up.* New York. Harper Collins.
[3] Polajnar D. (2021). *7 Unicorn Drive.* Cyprus. Login5 Aphrodite Ltd.
[4] https://www.linkedin.com/posts/andydavieshr_leadership-activity-6694682110747262976-Fnn6/
[5] https://www.psychologytoday.com/gb/basics/resilience
[6] https://thefutureorganization.com/former-ceo-of-ge-jeff-immelt-on-lessons-learned-working-with-jack-welch-dealing-with-critics/
[7] https://www2.deloitte.com/content/dam/Deloitte/pl/Documents/Reports/pl_Leaders_for_Today_Leaders_for_Tomorrow_EN_2014.pdf
[8] https://www2.deloitte.com/us/en/insights/focus/human-capital-trends/2019/21st-century-leadership-challenges-and-development.html
[9] https://www.britannica.com/technology/Moores-law
[10] Chernobyl - 2019 Sky Atlantic Drama https://www.amazon.co.uk/dp/B07RR73LT6/ref=cm_sw_em_r_mt_dp_hAtqFbC2S07BR
[11] Greenleaf. (1977). *Servant Leadership [25th Anniversary Edition]: A Journey into the Nature of Legitimate Power and Greatness.* Paulist Press. New York.
[12] Hesse H. (2016). *Journey to the East.* Owen: London.
[13] https://hbr.org/2018/04/how-humble-leadership-really-works
[14] https://www.linkedin.com/in/garryturnerstrategicadvisor/
[15] https://www.youtube.com/channel/UCEFGe1UOKrDpQol7-M795Zw
[16] https://www.skillpacks.com/servant-leadership-examples-in-business/
[17] https://www.forbes.com/sites/katecooper/2018/07/03/who-is-the-servant-leader-really-serving/?sh=5060c99d323c
[18] https://www.vogue.co.uk/news/article/jacinda-ardern-leadership-Approach
[19] Dan Price tweet dated 24 May 2021 https://twitter.com/DanPriceSeattle/status/1396622446233542670
[20] James Timpson tweet dated 26 April 2021 https://twitter.com/JamesTCobbler/status/1386618339288567815
[21] Covey S. (2020). *The 7 Habits Of Highly Effective People.* New York. Simon & Schuster.
[22] https://www.forbes.com/sites/jeffbercovici/2013/12/16/the-fatal-error-that-doomed-aols-patch/?sh=5e08731c38dc
[23] https://www.inc.com/justin-bariso/tumblr-ceo-david-karp-sent-an-extraordinary-email-to-employees-emotional-intelligence.html
[24] https://www.fnlondon.com/articles/read-andrea-orcels-farewell-message-to-ubs-staff-20180927
[25] https://www.cnbc.com/2017/06/13/marissa-mayers-goodbye-letter-to-yahoo.html
[26] https://www.express.co.uk/finance/city/1392585/jeff-bezos-resigns-amazon-

chief-sends-letter-to-staff-message-in-full-after-exit-evg
[27] https://www.edelman.com/trust/2021-trust-barometer
[28] Ulrich D. (2017). *Victory through Organisations*. New York. McGraw-Hill.
[29] https://www.glassdoor.co.uk/blog/best-places-to-work-2021-uk/
[30] https://www2.deloitte.com/content/dam/Deloitte/global/Documents/About-Deloitte/gx-core-beliefs-and-culture.pdf
[31] https://www.forbes.com/sites/johnkotter/2011/02/10/does-corporate-culture-drive-financial-performance/?sh=3752e9b67e9e
[32] https://hbr.org/2016/07/a-global-survey-on-the-ambiguous-state-of-employee-trust
[33] https://www.yeself.com/2020/12/10/7-stats-that-will-convince-you-of-the-crucial-role-of-corporate-culture/
[34] https://libertymind.co.uk/company-culture/
[35] https://www.ox.ac.uk/news/2019-10-24-happy-workers-are-13-more-productive
[36] https://www.indeed.com/hire/c/info/hook-candidates-with-your-company-culture-description
[37] https://www.gallup.com/workplace/229832/culture.aspx
[38] Sutton R. (2010). *The No Asshole Rule: Building a Civilized Workplace and Surviving One That Isn't*. USA. Piatkus.
[39] https://au.finance.yahoo.com/news/arianna-huffington-ams-015817689.html
[40] https://www.slideshare.net/reed2001/culture-2009/24-Imagine_if_every_person_at
[41] https://www.sonymusic.co.uk/about/culture/
[42] https://www.lenovo.com/gb/en/lenovo/our-culture/
[43] https://s3.amazonaws.com/rei-fyb/HR_Benefits_v2_18.04.23.pdf
[44] https://www.adobe.com/careers/why-adobe.html
[45] https://www.atlassian.com/blog/leadership/15-company-culture-examples-that-deserve-your-attention
[46] https://www.glassdoor.co.uk/blog/21732-2/
[47] https://www.bbc.co.uk/news/business-42791079
[48] https://www.bbc.co.uk/news/business-42779698
[49] https://bizfluent.com/facts-6887850-nike-s-flat-organizational-structure.html
[50] https://app.gumroad.com/about
[51] https://rankingdigitalrights.org/index2018/
[52] https://blog.volkovlaw.com/2020/05/the-boeing-scandal-and-the-demise-of-a-corporate-culture-part-i-of-iii/
[53] https://www.legislation.gov.uk/ukpga/2011/20/part/1/chapter/8
[54] https://www.techtimes.com/articles/251556/20200804/blizzard-employees-are-revolting-against-company-for-unequal-wages-shares-their-salaries.htm
[55] https://www.dfeh.ca.gov/wp-content/uploads/sites/32/2021/07/BlizzardPR.7.21.21.pdf
[56] https://www.bbc.co.uk/news/technology-58061231

[57] https://news.blizzard.com/en-us/blizzard/23706475/new-leadership-at-blizzard
[58] https://www.linkedin.com/pulse/why-one-most-powerful-questions-professionals-should-able-andy-davies/
[59] https://www.amazon.co.uk/Exploring-Strategy-Cases-Gerry-Johnson/dp/1292145129
[60] Kotter J P. (1996). *Leading Change.* USA. HBS Press.
[61] https://www.forbes.com/sites/sallypercy/2019/03/13/why-do-change-programs-fail/?sh=64cd34a82e48
[62] Burns B. (2004). *Managing Change*. London: Person Hall.
[63] Woodward and Buchholz. (1987). *Aftershock: Helping people through corporate change*. USA. Wiley.
[64] Petzer M. (2020). How to limit 'the sinking ship syndrome' during redundancies. Accessed on CIPD at https://www.cipd.co.uk/news-views/changing-work-views/future-work/thought-pieces/sinking-ships-syndrome-redundancies
[65] https://d16cvnquvjw7pr.cloudfront.net/resources/whitepapers/Zendesk_WP_Customer_Service_and_Business_Results.pdf
[66] https://www.superoffice.com/blog/customer-experience-statistics/
[67] https://thedijuliusgroup.com/
[68] https://www.bbc.co.uk/news/business-23058844
[69] Morgan J. (2014). *The Future of Work: Attract New Talent, Build Better Leaders, and Create a Competitive Organization.* USA. Wiley.
[70] https://www.bbc.co.uk/news/technology-23943480
[71] Morgan B. (2019). *Customer of the Future: 10 Guiding Principles for Winning Tomorrow's Business*. USA. Harper Collins.
[72] https://www.netpromoter.com/know/
[73] https://www.dailymail.co.uk/sport/olympics/article-9874753/Team-GBs-Chef-mission-Mark-England-hails-greatest-achievement-British-Olympic-history.html
[74] https://www.statista.com/statistics/193136/total-assets-of-the-walt-disney-company-since-2006
[75] Flow. (2002). Csikszentmihalyi M. Rider. London
[76] https://www.mckinsey.com/business-functions/organization/our-insights/the-organization-blog/6-elements-to-create-a-high-performing-culture
[77] https://www.forbes.com/sites/ashiraprossack1/2021/01/31/5-key-characteristics-of-high-performing-teams/?sh=516b23b3351d
[78] Gilbert T. (1996). *Human Performance*. Massachusetts. HRD Press.
[79] https://www.verywellmind.com/imposter-syndrome-and-social-anxiety-disorder-4156469
[80] https://www.birminghammail.co.uk/news/midlands-news/west-midlands-mayor-andy-street-21750089
[81] https://theconversation.com/whats-wrong-with-manels-and-what-can-we-do-about-them-148068
[82] https://corporate-rebels.com/buurtzorg-team-roles/

[83] https://www.zappos.com/about/how-we-work
[84] https://www.zapposinsights.com/about/holacracy?utm_campaign=newsroom&utm_medium=about-us&utm_source=how-we-work&utm_content=holacracy
[85] https://www.statista.com/study/65907/zapposcom-store-analysis/
[86] https://www.haier.com/index.html
[87] https://www.slideshare.net/londonbusinessschool/success-based-on-five-foundations-london-business-school/5-5Case_studyHaiers_80000_or_soemployees
[88] https://www.listennotes.com/podcasts/level-up-engineering/building-self-managed-teams-q-YIvE7azxr/
[89] Goleman D. 2003. *The New Leaders*. London. Sphere.
[90] Gladwell M. 2000. *The Tipping Point*. London. Abacus.
[91] https://www.forbes.com/connect/
[92] https://www.forbes.com/sites/forbespr/2020/10/14/forbes-launches-ceo-network-to-connect-inform-and-inspire-the-ceos-shaping-the-future-of-business/?sh=26bc4eef4b5b
[93] https://www.sportbible.com/football/news-reactions-phil-foden-sacks-social-media-company-after-tweet-about-kylian-mbappe-20210416
[94] https://www.out.com/news/2021/4/28/ceo-fired-after-publicly-harassing-teen-boy-wearing-dress-prom
[95] https://finance.yahoo.com/news/tesla-investor-sues-musk-says-180633617.html
[96] https://www.kellogg.northwestern.edu/faculty/uzzi/ftp/teaching%20materials/Example_std_papers/LeadershipNetworks_EMP70.pdf
[97] https://www.wired.co.uk/article/iceland-four-day-work-week
[98] https://www.bbc.co.uk/news/explainers-58626935
[99] https://www.businessinsider.com/the-rise-and-fall-of-blockbuster-video-streaming-2020-1?r=US&IR=T
[100] https://twitter.com/Procurement2030
[101] https://en.wikipedia.org/wiki/Autonomous_spaceport_drone_ship
[102] https://www.wired.com/story/john-deere-doubles-silicon-valley-robots/
[103] https://www.pwc.com/gx/en/services/people-organisation/publications/workforce-of-the-future.html
[104] https://www.finance101.com/robots/

Made in the USA
Monee, IL
12 November 2026

26ed0bd9-2eef-40d1-be42-da6bba928decR01